PRAISE FOR

UNSHAKABLE FAITH

"Aaron Graham has written the kind of book we desperately need right now—clear enough to cut through cultural fog, bold enough to confront the lies discipling a generation, and pastoral enough to heal the hearts those lies have harmed. With biblical conviction and Christlike compassion, he shows us how to follow Jesus without compromise and love the world without losing ourselves. This book is a road map for anyone who wants an authentic, resilient faith in an age of noise, nonsense, and nuance."

—Dharius Daniels, D.Min, lead pastor at Change Church and author of *Relational Intelligence*

"Aaron Graham's voice is Gospel-centered, wise, and steady. His new book, *Unshakable Faith,* is a helpful guide for navigating the days we've been entrusted with and the culture in which we live."

—Annie F. Downs, *New York Times* bestselling author of *That Sounds Fun*

"Reading *Unshakable Faith* feels like standing at the intersection of C. S. Lewis, John Perkins, and Tim Keller. Aaron Graham engages secular progressivism with conviction, but never with contempt. His tone is thoughtful, gracious, and true. Most of all, his writing is saturated with the gospel and a heart for discipleship. This is the kind of book that steadies anxious hearts, sharpens faithful minds, and helps followers of Jesus pursue holiness and speak with courage and kindness in a confusing age. *Unshakable Faith* is deeply needed for this generation."

—Derwin L. Gray, co-founder and lead pastor of Transformation Church and author of *Lit Up with Love*

"*Unshakable Faith* is the most timely and relevant book addressing the personal, communal, and cultural challenges facing the church today. With courage and clarity, it exposes prevailing lies and inconsistencies, and it confronts them with compelling, timeless truths rooted in the Word of God and the power of the Holy Spirit. This book enlivens us—both individually and collectively—to rise up, embrace true worship, reclaim our identity in Christ, and fulfill our earthly mandate by pursuing justice with sacrificial love for the most vulnerable. I applaud Pastor Aaron Graham for boldly calling us out with a rare blend of urgency, conviction, and compassion."

—Ndidi Okonkwo Nwuneli, president and CEO of the ONE Campaign

"Aaron Graham nails it with *Unshakable Faith,* bringing a much-needed message of clarity and focus in a divisive age of echo chambers—where no one listens, everyone virtue signals, and a plethora of good things too often unintentionally end up superseding the most important thing. This is a book that needs to be widely read and, more important, put into practice by all those who call themselves Jesus followers."

—Larry Osborne, D.Min., author and pastor at North Coast Church

"Not only is Aaron Graham a friend whom I love and respect, but we also have the joy of serving the same city. Aaron is a deep well of wisdom. This book will stretch your faith and deepen it at the same time. Both timeless and timely, *Unshakable Faith* will help you rediscover faith with your fingerprint on it."

—Mark Batterson, *New York Times* bestselling author of *The Circle Maker*

"Aaron delivers one of the most insightful and balanced explorations of faith and truth in changing times. *Unshakable Faith* clarifies and reinforces kingdom culture, provokes a deep hunger for Jesus, and is a catalyst for revival in a non-intrusive yet compelling manner."

—Godman Akinlabi, global lead pastor at The Elevation Church in Lagos, Nigeria, and author of *The Seven Commandments of Foolishness*

"In *Unshakable Faith,* Aaron Graham calls out the important cultural lies that have distorted the gospel message today. The issues he discusses would once been particular to the Western church, but today they confront a rising generation of African and global Christian youth who share a common digital culture. Rather than reacting in fear or retreat, this book shows how time-tested, Spirit-formed practices can anchor our faith in truth and help us engage our world with courage. I wholeheartedly recommend this book to pastors and leaders across the world who, like myself, are seeking to preach the gospel with clarity, faithfulness, and relevance to today's generation."

—Muriithi Wanjau, senior pastor of the Mavuno Church Movement

"*Unshakable Faith* is a bold declaration of war against seven lies that can easily take our mind and spirit hostage. This powerful work belongs in the hands of anyone who desires a closer, more vibrant, spirit-filled walk with God. Dr. Graham has rightly issued a *must-read* clarion call for God's people as we run toward "the kingdom that cannot be shaken," standing firm against the lies of the world and boldly proclaiming the message of the only One who saves."

—Adam C. Wright, Ph.D., president at Dallas Baptist University

UNSHAKABLE FAITH

AARON GRAHAM

UNSHAKABLE FAITH

HOW TO STAND FIRM IN A CULTURE OF LIES

MULTNOMAH

Multnomah
An imprint of the Penguin Random House Christian Publishing Group,
a division of Penguin Random House LLC
1745 Broadway, New York, NY 10019
waterbrookmultnomah.com
penguinrandomhouse.com

Italics in Scripture quotations reflect the author's added emphasis.

LIBRARY OF CONGRESS CATALOGING-IN-PUBLICATION DATA
Names: Graham, Aaron, Pastor author
Title: Unshakable faith / Aaron Graham.
Description: New York, NY: Multnomah, 2026 | Includes bibliographical references.
Identifiers: LCCN 2025040656 (print) | LCCN 2025040657 (ebook) |
ISBN 9798217151592 hardcover | ISBN 9798217151608 ebook
Subjects: LCSH: Faith (Christianity) | Christian life
Classification: LCC BV4637.G648 2026 (print) | LCC BV4637 (ebook)
LC record available at https://lccn.loc.gov/2025040656
LC ebook record available at https://lccn.loc.gov/2025040657

Printed in the United States of America

1st Printing

First Edition

The authorized representative in the EU for product safety and compliance is Penguin Random House Ireland, Morrison Chambers, 32 Nassau Street, Dublin D02 YH68, Ireland.
https://eu-contact.penguin.ie

BOOKMAKING TEAM: Production editor: Jocelyn Kiker • Managing editor: Julia Wallace •
Production manager: Chanler Harris • Copy editor: Lisa Grimenstein •
Proofreaders: Debbie Anderson, Emily Cutler

To the people of The District Church,

who have dared to believe that revival is possible—

even in our nation's capital.

This book reflects your faith and courage.

May you continue to stand firm in the gospel.

My dear brothers and sisters, *stand firm.* Let nothing move you. Always give yourselves fully to the work of the Lord, because you know that your labor in the Lord is not in vain.

—1 Corinthians 15:58

FOREWORD

If I could sum up *Unshakable Faith* in three words, they would be *urgency, potency,* and *possibility.* It feels less like a book and more like a prophetic summons for the church in our time, and this needed summons comes from a voice I deeply trust and respect. I have known Aaron Graham for over a decade and count it a privilege to write this foreword, having long admired the consistency of his life and the clarity of his calling. He is one of those rare leaders who can hold together conviction and compassion, intellect and intimacy with God, faithfulness to Scripture and faithfulness to his people. And he has done this in one of the most complex and power-driven cities in the world—Washington, D.C.—with defiant joy.

When I had the honor of preaching at The District Church, I saw what Aaron describes in these pages happening right in front of me. It was a diverse church, with faces from every background and stories from almost every continent, worshiping together in unity. It was a deep church, marked by teaching that didn't flinch from truth but was clearly rooted in love. And it was a visionary church, alive with expectation that the gospel could renew even the nation's capital. That morning, I remember thinking, *Many people write about the idea of planting and leading a missional church, but Aaron has actually done it.* The themes that fill this book—discernment, courage, and conviction—were already living and breathing in that room, a living parable right in front of me.

Aaron is not a theorist; he's a practitioner. His theology has been shaped in the crucible of pastoring people through the cultural turbulence of our age. What defines him is not his pedigree but his fruit. He has seen God move through his life, his church, and his city in ways that no seminary degree or master's degree from an Ivy League school could produce. He has built ministries that care for the poor, disciple young professionals, and unite churches across divides that usually fracture communities. His life is the best argument for everything he writes here, and I cannot stress how important this is in a world that so often offers specific critiques with vague solutions.

As you read, you feel a sense of urgency in *Unshakable Faith* because Aaron knows what's at stake. He has seen too many people drift from conviction into confusion, too many churches lose depth in their chase for relevance, and too many believers underestimate the cultural forces shaping their souls. This book is his response—a call to resist the slow secularization of the church by returning to a rooted faith in Christ. But this book was not written in despair; it is filled with possibility. Every chapter is infused with hope that the same Spirit who sustained the early church can strengthen us again today.

This is not a nostalgic book about reclaiming the past. It's a prophetic book about preparing for the future. Aaron exposes the lies that have seeped into modern Christianity, but he doesn't stop there—he offers a path forward. The pairing of lies with counter-practices gives this book its potency. It doesn't just critique; it offers a vision of formation. And it doesn't simply warn; it empowers you to respond.

Having seen Aaron's ministry up close, I can assure you

that he is neither trying to impress the culture nor retreat from it. He is standing within it, full of resolve and love. The result is a model of what discipleship can look like in an age of compromise, offering a vision of what faithfulness can be when it's anchored in Scripture, empowered by the Spirit, and lived for the good of the world.

And in this sense, *Unshakable Faith* is more than a book; it lays a foundation of counter-formation for a generation wanting more. It is a manifesto for those who still believe that the gospel can transform people and cities. It is urgent because time is short. It is potent because it is rooted in truth. And it is full of possibility because it flows from the heart of a pastor who believes revival is still possible.

This book is not just written for Washington, D.C.; it's written for every follower of Jesus trying to remain faithful in a world that keeps shifting. And if you take its message seriously, it might just form in you the kind of faith our world needs most and we all long to have—an unshakable one.

Jon Tyson
Pastor and author
Church of the City New York

CONTENTS

WHEN TRUTH GETS TWISTED

How Secular Culture Is Rewriting Christianity from Within

> My dear Wormwood, I note with grave displeasure that your patient has become a Christian . . . There is no need to despair; hundreds of these adult converts have been reclaimed after a brief sojourn in the Enemy's camp and are now with us.
>
> —*The Screwtape Letters,* Letter 2

A few years ago, I was trying to enjoy a long-awaited vacation, but I couldn't. Names kept flooding my mind: Friends from high school. College classmates. Ministry peers. People who once followed Jesus passionately but had since drifted away.

Eventually, I gave up trying to block it out. I grabbed a notebook and started writing down names, one after another and page after page. As the list grew, so did the ache inside me. Eventually I put down my pen and wept.

So. Many. Names. And this list was just my peers, people I had grown up with and served alongside. It didn't include those I've pastored over the last twenty years. That list would be much longer.

For decades I've watched too many of God's people walk away. Again and again, I find myself weeping and praying that they would turn back to the God who is waiting to receive them with open arms.

I've written this book because I'm on a mission to stop the drift. To help our generation develop an unshakable faith. To help you discern the lies our culture keeps feeding us.

But before I go any further, I need to make a confession: I've been part of the problem.

THE DISCIPLESHIP CRISIS

I used to think my job as a pastor was simple. Get people in the door. Win them to Christ. Connect them to a small group. Lovingly serve our city. I thought if my church did these things with excellence, we would influence our city for Christ.

But here's what I learned: It doesn't matter how many people you get through the front door if you aren't concerned about how many are walking out the back.

Many Christians are compromising their faith or leaving it altogether—not because they've rejected Jesus outright, but because they're being shaped more by *secular culture* than by the historic Christian faith. In other words, they are becoming secularized "Christians"—still professing Christ, but being shaped more by culture than Scripture.

And while there are many places to point the blame, pastors like me have been chief among them. We have often failed to take seriously the slow, subtle way the world steps in where the church steps back.

What I've come to realize is this: *If the church doesn't disciple people, the world gladly will.*

And right now, the world is doing a better job.

Every year, millions walk away from their faith in Jesus.[1] And although it's more difficult to track, the number of people who still call themselves Christians while compromising the core teachings of Christianity is even greater.

I don't know about you, but as a family member, friend, pastor, and most important, follower of Jesus, I am burdened.

War is being waged. It's not a physical war fought with weapons. It's not a culture war fought with clickbait or sound bites. It's a spiritual war—fought over what is true and false regarding the one true and living God.

And the battlefield? It's the hearts and minds of people in my church and city, and in yours.

Although I know how the war ends (Revelation 12:10–11), I am burdened because, many days, it feels like we are losing.

Casualties are stacking up. And I don't want you—or the people you love—to become one of them.

WHERE I WENT WRONG

For much of my ministry, I thought the main challenge was making the gospel relevant.

I believed that if we emphasized our justice and mercy work—if we showed we cared about the poor, the city, the hurting—then people would see Christianity as credible. I especially thought this plan would work in a place like D.C., where people are highly educated and deeply engaged in issues of justice. I thought, if we could just prove we care about what people care about, they'd be more open to Jesus.

But here's where I went wrong: Relevance isn't the same as faithfulness.

In my efforts to make the gospel feel accessible and inoffensive, I unintentionally softened its edges. Under my influence, my church highlighted the parts of faith that aligned with cultural values and downplayed the parts that required deep repentance or countercultural obedience. We gave people a vision for how Christianity could fit into their lives, rather than calling them to reorient their entire lives around Christ.

And this doesn't just happen from the pulpit. Many of us, especially young Christians, feel the pressure to present a version of our faith that will be accepted by our peers. We curate our beliefs on social media to seem thoughtful, not offensive.

We avoid hard conversations. We want to be known as loving and inclusive, not judgmental or narrow-minded. And in the process, we often end up living a faith that's more about image than about truth.

Let me be clear: I'm not saying we need fewer justice ministries or more boring church services. I'm not calling for harsh, judgmental Christianity that repels more than it invites. What I am saying is this: In our effort to make faith more culturally relevant, we've too often compromised the very truths that make it transformative.

Faithfulness to Jesus requires compassion and conviction. But when we elevate cultural acceptance above biblical allegiance, we end up reshaping the gospel to fit the moment—rather than proclaiming the truth that transcends every moment.

And over time, that compromise creates a vacuum. We begin to neglect deep discipleship. We stop asking hard questions. And as a result, many look elsewhere for answers—not from mature spiritual mentors, but from Instagram therapists, TikTok influencers, or cynical deconstruction threads on Reddit.

Lies then flood into this discipleship void—and sadly, many come from *within the church*. The most dangerous lies are often the ones that sound the most compassionate, the most modern, the most "Christian." Sometimes they're even preached from the pulpit.

The consequences of this softening aren't theoretical; they're deeply personal. I've seen it play out in the lives of people I care about. Despite our best intentions, the faith we modeled and taught wasn't always deep enough to anchor them when the cultural currents shifted. It wasn't that they stopped believing overnight. It was slower, subtler. A quiet drift that started with good intentions but ended in a faith unrecognizable from the one they once proclaimed.

I remember a young leader I mentored years ago—passionate, smart, and very committed to serving. He served eagerly and soaked up everything we taught. But over time, I started noticing subtle changes. His social media posts gradually shifted—less Scripture, more activism. He stopped attending church regularly, saying he could connect with God just as easily through nature or a podcast. When I reached out, he told me he still loved Jesus, but no longer felt aligned with "organized religion."

A few years later, he told me he was reevaluating *everything*. He hadn't rejected Jesus, at least not in name. But the Jesus he now followed looked less like the one in the Gospels and more like a vague spiritual guide who affirmed all his choices. He didn't walk away in one dramatic moment—it happened gradually, almost imperceptibly. As his pastor and friend, I couldn't help but wonder: Had we discipled him well? Had we articulated a deep enough faith that was resilient to stand up to cultural pressure?

THE LIES THAT FILL THE VOID

When we started as a church, my mentor and leadership guru, Pastor Steve Stroope, sent me a sample job description for my role as a pastor. The first responsibility listed in the long description was this: "The Lead Pastor is to protect the congregation from false teaching" (Acts 20:28).

At the time, I thought I could skip over that part. Other parts of the job description felt more urgent—facilities, finances, outreach, evangelism. *Besides,* I thought, *I pastor a church in the most educated city in the world. Our people are smart. They're responsible and articulate. Many of them grew up in church. If they didn't, they're fast learners. Surely, they can discern false teaching on their own.* But as I reflect on the number of people who have drifted from their relationship with God, I'm reminded why this calling—to resist false teaching—is so important.

Jesus warned us in Matthew 7:15–16, "Watch out for false prophets. They come to you in sheep's clothing, but inwardly they are ferocious wolves. By their fruit you will recognize them."

Jesus' warning troubles me for several reasons.

First, these false prophets are not outside the church—they're *in it.* Earlier in the Sermon on the Mount, Jesus warned about persecution from outside: "Blessed are those who are persecuted because of righteousness" (Matthew 5:10). But here, the danger is from within.

Second, Jesus called them *prophets.* These aren't just church attendees—they're church *leaders.* False teaching isn't just present—it's platformed. It's in our small groups, our discipleship classes, our pulpits.

Third, Jesus said they're *ferocious wolves.* They might appear to have good intentions, but their teaching will wound you. Jesus later said, "I am sending you out like sheep among wolves" (Matthew 10:16). Paul echoed these words in his farewell speech to the Ephesian elders: "I know that after I leave, savage wolves will come in among you and will not spare the flock" (Acts 20:29).

There are wolves in the church, and they are hunting sheep.

Finally—and perhaps most disturbing—Jesus said they come in *sheep's clothing.* They disguise themselves. They look like everyone else.[2] They speak truth—*mostly.* It's been said the biggest lies contain a surprising amount of truth. A message can be 90 percent correct and still be built around one soul-destroying lie. That's what makes false teaching so hard to discern: You find yourself amening so many things they say.

This has always been the enemy's strategy. He mixes truth with lies.

It's how he tempted Jesus in the wilderness—with Scripture, twisted Scripture. Paul warned the Corinthian church: "Satan himself masquerades as an angel of light. It is not surprising, then, if his servants also masquerade as servants of righteousness" (2 Corinthians 11:14–15).

We must be careful and discerning. Just because someone has a mic, a book deal, a stage, or a verified account does not mean their words are trustworthy. False prophets are the original deepfake.

So how do we spot false teaching? How do we keep from being led astray?

Much of this book is devoted to those very questions—helping you peel back the religious veneer and confront what's really being taught. Even more important, helping you return to the beautiful, unshakable truth of the real Jesus, who makes the Christian faith so compelling, beautiful, and transformative.

EXPRESSIVE INDIVIDUALISM

The enemy's lies don't appear in a vacuum. They are delivered through culture—and one of the primary delivery systems today is what sociologists call "expressive individualism."

Sociologist Robert Bellah, who wrote *Habits of the Heart,*

coined this phrase.[3] It's the belief that authority lies within your own experience and interpretation of the truth. You get to decide for yourself what is best and morally good. Each person has their own path to truth. The chief goal in life becomes your own happiness, your own version of truth, your own experience. Authority rests in your feelings, rather than a universal truth that applies to everyone.

These messages are packaged in slogans we've heard a thousand times—harmless on the surface, but deeply formative beneath:

- *"You be you."* As Beyoncé said, "Your self-worth is determined by you. You don't have to depend on someone telling you who you are."[4]
- *"Follow your heart."* Joel Osteen writes, "You have to learn to follow your heart. You can't let other people pressure you into being something that you're not."[5]
- *"Live your truth."* As Glennon Doyle—who publicly walked away from her Christian faith—writes in *Untamed:* "Maybe Eve was never meant to be our warning. Maybe she was meant to be our model. Own your wanting. Eat the apple. Let it burn."[6]

In *Disappearing Church,* Mark Sayers describes the beliefs that thrive in this environment.[7] At its core expressive individualism is the conviction that individual freedom is the highest good. Anything that restricts that freedom—tradition, religion, even biology—is seen as oppressive and must be dismantled. People are assumed to be inherently good, so if everyone just follows their inner voice, society will naturally improve. In this framework, tolerance becomes the chief virtue, especially when it comes to affirming someone's self-defined identity and personal expression. Institutions are met with suspicion, and any form of external authority is rejected. The authentic self reigns supreme.

The problem is, when autonomy becomes your highest good, following Jesus becomes impossible—because He said: "Whoever wants to be my disciple must deny themselves and take up their cross and follow me" (Matthew 16:24).

Autonomy was the original sin in Genesis 3. The serpent's question—"Did God really say . . . ?"—invited Adam and Eve to become their own judges of truth, to trust their own fleshly desires over God's commands. That's the same temptation we face today: Will we take God at His word, or bend the truth to fit how we feel?

When autonomy becomes your highest good, following Jesus becomes impossible.

This cultural emphasis on expressive individualism doesn't just reshape how we relate to institutions or authority; it reshapes our understanding of faith itself. When personal experience and self-expression become the ultimate measures of truth, traditional beliefs naturally come under scrutiny—and sometimes rejection. It's within this environment that a new form of faith emerges, one commonly referred to as "progressive Christianity."

WHAT IS A PROGRESSIVE CHRISTIAN?

Let me be clear—by "progressive Christian," I don't mean someone who is politically progressive.

I'm talking about someone who reinterprets Scripture and

the historic teachings of the church to make them more acceptable to modern culture—or more comfortable for themselves. It often starts with good intentions: making the gospel "relevant."

That was me, especially early in ministry—overlooking the importance of training young Christians in the core tenets of the Christian faith. Instead, I focused on mobilizing them toward action. But what I didn't realize was that the cultural winds beneath us were already shifting. I could no longer assume that the church was defending the foundational truths of Christianity. In fact, there were growing forces—even within the church—working to *change* those core beliefs.

Progressive Christianity often emphasizes the urgency of compassionately loving our neighbor, while downplaying—or even rejecting—core doctrine related to submitting to God's authority and holiness. And that's how the enemy works. He sows weeds among the wheat. He mixes subtle lies with good intentions.

It almost always starts the same way: a slow departure from the historic Christian faith.

Someone says they're looking for a more progressive church—one that better reflects their views on human sexuality, or one that prioritizes racial justice. But when I check in years later, most of these increasingly progressive Christians aren't committed to a local church any longer. They may still call themselves Christians, but they no longer practice their faith—except to fiercely defend the moral framework of expressive individualism.

At first, I thought progressive Christianity was just about different views on hot-button issues like sexuality. But over time, I've learned it's far more. In many cases, progressive Christianity has become the gateway drug for post-Christianity.

THE RISE OF THE THIRD CULTURE

Philip Rieff, a secular sociologist and cultural commentator, described three types of culture.[8] This framework has helped me understand what's happening spiritually and culturally in our time.

1. **First Culture**—Belief in many gods.

   These are pre-Christian societies. People are spiritual and moral. They believe in good and evil. There's a sense of cosmic order and the need to keep the gods happy. This has been the dominant worldview in most of human history.
2. **Second Culture**—Belief in one God.

   These are Judeo-Christian cultures rooted in Scripture. They believe God has revealed a rational and sacred order to the universe. Morality is grounded in divine commandments. Peace, security, and human flourishing come from worshiping and obeying the one true God.
3. **Third Culture**—The god of self.

   This is our post-Christian world. It defines itself in opposition to the second culture. There is no greater truth. The sacred is deconstructed. The goal is to dismantle all moral boundaries and sacred prohibitions that threaten personal autonomy. Authority lies not in God, but in the self. Everything is contested and reinterpreted through personal experience.[9]

As Rieff saw it, each culture isn't just different—they're in tension. And the tension is growing.

Yet most Christians are unaware of the spiritual danger these dynamics present.

The *danger for Christian second cultures* communicating the gospel *to first cultures* is that they may inadvertently *colonize* them. This has been the critique of some Western missionaries in the last few centuries—imposing cultural norms rather than simply proclaiming Christ.

But when *second-culture Christians* engage *third cultures,* the danger is reversed: They risk being *colonized themselves*—absorbed into the mindset of the culture they're trying to reach.[10]

The third culture is not passive. It's deeply evangelistic—offering its own gospel, its own moral framework, and its own version of salvation. Despite presenting itself as inclusive, it doesn't tolerate alternate views, especially ones that come from the second culture. Instead, it aggressively promotes its own vision of truth, identity, and human flourishing.

In many ways, the third culture has become more committed to making disciples than the church today.

The evangelistic zeal of third cultures can be seen in how society redefines core ideas that were once grounded in Scripture and tradition. Marriage is no longer a covenant rooted in biblical design, but a vehicle for personal expression. Justice is no longer anchored in righteousness and right relationships, but reshaped into performative action or partisan alignment. Even gender identity—once grounded in biology and community—is now fluid, determined by inner feelings.

In each case, the source of authority has shifted: from God to self.

This is where discernment becomes absolutely critical.

Many Christians today are slowly transitioning into the third culture without even realizing it. Why? Because they still speak the language of the second. They were raised in it. They know how to sound biblical. They still talk about Jesus, love, and justice. But underneath, their worldview is being shaped by third-culture values—autonomy, self-expression, and personal truth. Their faith *looks* familiar, but it no longer operates from the same foundation.

And this is where progressive Christianity often enters in.

FROM PROGRESSIVE CHRISTIANITY TO POST-CHRISTIANITY

For many, progressive Christianity becomes a layover—a transitional phase between the second and third cultures. It still sounds Christian. It still uses Christian language. But it gradually softens, edits, or redefines core beliefs to stay aligned with the values of the third culture.

John Mark Comer captures this dynamic well when he says: "In my pastoral experience . . . progressive Christianity, not for all people but for most, is a stopover on the way to post-Christianity. Because it can't hold any robust discipleship. Because it has no ethical stance against the world."[11]

This is the heart of the problem with progressive Christianity. Many Christians think they are being strategic or inclusive by compromising on certain doctrines to evangelize the third culture. But in reality, they are *being* evangelized. In an effort to engage culture, they become co-opted by it. Let me make it personal: You are being evangelized—daily, if not hourly—by a culture that wants you to compromise your faith.

In my experience, progressive Christians often risk becoming more shaped by progressivism than by historic Christianity. The desire to remain relevant to culture can gradually outweigh faithfulness to Scripture and to God.

As a people pleaser—and someone who deeply desires to reach people who are far from God—I know the temptation to soften the edges, to make truth more palatable, to trade clarity for connection. But if I'm not careful, that desire to reach others can quietly erode core biblical convictions.

It's true that if you want to lead someone to faith, you have to earn their trust—by showing how much you care, meeting real human needs, and speaking to the issues they care about. But here's the danger: When relevance becomes the highest goal, it won't be long until faithfulness is watered down.

Lies get embedded in our belief systems gradually. We take a good and important principle—like being welcoming, loving, or "doing whatever it takes to help someone feel seen"—and we make it the ultimate goal. Even if it means compromising core biblical truth. But here's the thing: We rarely recognize these moves as compromises. We assume we're being faithful. We convince ourselves that we're just being compassionate, just trying to reach people, just keeping an open mind. All the while, something foundational begins to shift.

There is a spiritual warfare aspect to this, of discerning truth from lies. The enemy will wear people down, but he does this so gradually that we hardly notice. People often compromise one belief at a time until the enemy has his way. In time they either deny their faith entirely or call themselves "Christians" while they retain less and less of the historic commitments until there is almost nothing noticeably Christian about their worldview anymore.[12]

THE SLOW DRIFT TO DENIAL

This trend is nothing new. Progressive Christian theology has been shaping the West for the past five hundred years. Roger Olson's lengthy *The Journey of Modern Theology* traces the long arc of this shift.[13] But today, there is a riptide of deconstruction that is growing stronger and stronger each year, and it's pulling many out of the church and into a sea of secularism.

One of the patterns Olson highlights is that progressive Christians usually end up denying the miraculous. He describes the miraculous as God working in supernatural ways that defy science and human comprehension.[14] And this matters—because Christians, by definition, believe in supernatural ministry, the gifts of the Spirit, miraculous healing, and most important one specific miracle that is absolutely central to our faith: the resurrection of Jesus.

This cosmic event stands at the very center of Christianity. Everything hinges on it. "If Christ has not been raised, your faith is futile; you are still in your sins" (1 Corinthians 15:17). If you do not believe in the bodily resurrection of Jesus, the Bible is clear: You are not a Christian.

We must be discerning. Remember, Jesus didn't say, "Watch out for false atheists, false agnostics, or false pagans." He said, "Watch out for false *prophets.*"

They are likely in your church. On your podcasts. On your bookshelves. And they sound a lot more convincing than you likely realize.

I've been around the block long enough to see many progressive Christians land in a place where they no longer believe the following:

- Christ is the only way to salvation.
- The Holy Spirit provides supernatural gifts.
- The Bible is the written Word of God.
- Heaven and hell are real places.
- We are sinful and need God.
- Christ's death on the cross accomplished something literal, not just metaphorical.

Keep poking holes in the gospel, and eventually you'll end up with a Bible full of them.

The enemy is deceiving millions—not through bold denials, but through a slow erosion of truth, one belief at a time.

It rarely happens in a moment. It's subtle. It's incremental. It's easy to miss until it's too late.

Over time, these compromises accumulate—until we either abandon our faith or continue calling ourselves "Christian" while believing almost nothing that actually defines it.

So how do we resist the drift? How do we spot these lies before they take root? And what does a faithful, healthy relationship with our culture look like?

THREE WAYS TO RESPOND TO CULTURE

In his classic book *Christ and Culture,* Richard Niebuhr presents five ways Christians have historically related to culture.[15] Here are three of the most familiar ones:

1. **Go Against Culture.** This is when you resist culture by separating from it or shouting at it. You rage about how the government, the schools, the media, and our laws don't reflect a Christian worldview. You critique from the sidelines, but you don't engage. You don't run for office. You don't show up in your local school. You don't offer a better vision on your social media. You just make noise from a distance.

   But righteous anger without redemptive action only hardens hearts. This posture may sound like boldness, but it often lacks love, wisdom, and discernment. There's a difference between contending for truth and simply venting frustration. The gospel doesn't call us to be culture warriors; it calls us to be ambassadors.

2. **Assimilate into Culture.** This is when you try to engage—but end up conforming. You reshape your core beliefs to fit dominant cultural narratives. Your desire for relevance has you sounding less like Scripture and more like the world. This is happening everywhere today and is a major reason I wrote this book.

   But cultural conformity isn't the only option. There's a better way—one that blends truth and love, conviction and compassion.

3. **Transform Culture.** This is when you engage culture faithfully—living in the world but not of it. You show up with both conviction and love. You go to the games, the museum, the coffee shop. You might even post a reel on Instagram. But you also draw clear lines. There are things you won't watch, won't comment on, won't participate in—because your purpose isn't popularity. It's transformation.

You can live in the world without becoming like the world.

Jesus commissioned us to make disciples of all nations. He commanded us to love our neighbors, especially those who don't believe what we believe. And He specifically prayed into this tension before going to the cross:

> My prayer is not that you take them out of the world but that you protect them from the evil one. They are not of the world, even as I am not of it. Sanctify them by

> the truth; your word is truth. As you sent me into the world, I have sent them into the world. (John 17:15–18)

Jesus is sending you *into* the world.

And He will not send you somewhere He won't also equip you to stand.

You can live in the world without becoming like the world.

You can engage culture *without compromise.*

THE SEVEN LIES—AND HOW TO DEFEAT THEM

If you sense the drift happening in you—or in the people you love—know this:

It does *not* have to continue.

You can get reconnected with a vibrant, truth-filled faith more powerful and enduring than the temptations surrounding you. Jesus promised He would never leave you or forsake you. He promised you can have a thriving faith—even in a secular age.[16]

The good news: We don't have to reinvent the wheel to learn how to be *in* the world but not *of* it. We are not the first to try.

For two thousand years, followers of Jesus have endured cultural pressure, spiritual deception, and even persecution—not by hiding or compromising, but by standing firm in the timeless practices that form an unshakable faith.

As Paul exhorted us, "Put on the full armor of God, so that you will be able to *stand firm* against the schemes of the devil" (Ephesians 6:11, NASB).

In the chapters ahead, we'll explore seven lies Christians often believe—each one deceptively spiritual but deeply corrosive to a vibrant life with God. These lies don't just remain abstract ideas. Over time, they shape the kind of people we become. They form distorted identities that masquerade as faithfulness, while quietly pulling us away from the way of Jesus.

These are the *counterfeit identities* that emerge when cultural lies go unchallenged in the church:

1. **The Self-Centered Worshiper** who drifts from God-centered devotion and makes faith about personal fulfillment.
2. **The Church Shopper** who treats church as optional and chooses comfort over deep community.
3. **The Lukewarm Believer** who keeps faith private instead of living with bold public witness.
4. **The Selective Christian** who edits Scripture to fit preferences rather than engaging the whole Word of God.
5. **The Armchair Activist** who champions causes online but resists the costly call to biblical justice.
6. **The Skeptical Believer** who replaces revelation with reason and resists the power of the Spirit.
7. **The Divisive Influencer** who mirrors cancel culture instead of practicing radical forgiveness and grace.

In each chapter, I'll not only name the lie and its subtle influence, but expose the identity it forms, and invite you into a better way. A truer way. One shaped not by culture but by Christ.

For each lie, we'll recover a historic spiritual practice—a way to ground our lives in truth and become the kind of people who can truly stand firm.

HISTORIC SPIRITUAL PRACTICES:

1. **True Worship**—an invitation to a renewed and God-centered faith
2. **Deep Community**—an invitation to be spiritually formed through the local church
3. **Bold Storytelling**—an invitation to share your faith with courage and authenticity
4. **Bible Engagement**—an invitation to dive deep into all of God's Word
5. **Biblical Justice**—an invitation to pursue justice with sacrificial love
6. **Spirit-Filled Living**—an invitation to discover and operate in your spiritual gifts
7. **Radical Forgiveness**—an invitation to practice peacemaking in a divided world

You can resist the lies of the enemy.

You can become a beacon of hope to those searching for truth.

You can follow Jesus and be truly authentic, engaged, loving, and unwavering.

But you must stay alert.

The enemy is cunning, and his lies have been refined over millennia of hating God and deceiving the human heart.

But take heart.

While you're about to see the playbook designed for your destruction, you'll also discover the practices to defeat its lies. Anchored in biblical truth, these practices will lead you to a faith that cannot be shaken.

UNSHAKABLE
FAITH

1

WHEN DEVOTION DRIFTS

From Self-Centered Faith to God-Centered Worship

> The best thing, where it is possible, is to keep the patient from the serious intention of praying altogether . . . the simplest is to turn their gaze away from Him towards themselves.
>
> —*The Screwtape Letters,* Letter 4

In 2008, I had the privilege of sitting down with Dr. James Lawson, one of the chief architects of the Civil Rights Movement.

Dr. Lawson founded the Student Nonviolent Coordinating Committee (SNCC) and championed the nonviolent protesting technique to Martin Luther King, Jr. I hung on his every word.

As we talked, he shared something that has shaped my life since: "Injustice is always justified with a big lie. The prophetic task of the church is to discern the lie and expose it."

He explained how he, Dr. King, Ella Baker, and others used to go into communities and conduct interviews to discern the root of racial injustice in our country. The first question they would ask was:

"What is the lie most people in this community believe?"

Gradually, they uncovered the big lie at the root of racial injustice: *Some people's lives are worth more than others.*

But underneath that belief was a deeper distortion—the

age-old tendency to place self at the center, above others and even above God.

Self-centered faith leads to compromised worship.

Racial injustice is rooted in self-centeredness—a sinful belief that my life, my comfort, and my advancement matter more than yours. It's the elevation of self over neighbor. And that's why addressing it required more than policy change—it required spiritual awakening.

So, Dr. Lawson and the others began asking a second critical question in those communities: "What is the spiritual *solution* to that lie?"

What they discovered was both theologically profound and nationally resonant. The antidote to the big lie of racial injustice was a foundational truth—one rooted in Genesis 1 and reflected in the best ideals of the U.S. Constitution.

The truth: All people are created equal.

From the opening pages of Scripture, we see that every human being is made in the image of God—the imago Dei—and therefore carries equal worth, dignity, and value. This truth, enshrined in the Constitution, became the moral and spiritual imperative behind the Civil Rights Movement.

Pastors and organizers addressed the foundational lie by appealing to two powerful sources of authority: Scripture and the Constitution. And in doing so, they reminded the nation that true justice begins with true worship—putting God, not self, at the center.

Sin runs rampant when lies pervade. Freedom and justice reign when we overcome lies with truth.

When we planted The District Church, we followed a similar playbook. We were not just starting a weekly service; we were seeking to build a church for the city. A church that would address the real, often unspoken, spiritual lies shaping people's lives. So we hit the streets and asked more than two hundred people two simple but revealing questions:

1. What is the lie most people in our city believe?
2. What is the spiritual solution to that lie?

What we heard back was incredibly consistent. The lie wasn't loud or obvious—but it was everywhere. It went something like this:

You can change the world on your own.

The problem facing our church was not that people were opposed to community. But there was a pervasive sense that community was optional. That what really mattered was individual effort—earning the right degrees, building the perfect résumé, making the right connections. Then, and only then, could you make a difference.

At first, this way of thinking sounded noble. Ambitious. Even inspiring. But as we considered it more deeply, we realized the problem wasn't just disconnection from others. The problem was a deeper spiritual drift—one that placed the self, rather than God, at the center.

That's the danger of unexamined cultural lies: they often sound like truth. But over time, they quietly reshape what we believe about purpose, success, and even God. And if we're not careful, they begin to inform not only how we live but how we worship.

THE LIE: IT'S ALL ABOUT ME

The first and most foundational lie Christians are tempted to believe today is: *It's all about me.*

We would never say it out loud. Few would ever claim to believe this lie directly. But it shows up—in our decisions, our prayers, our priorities.

We choose churches based on how they meet our needs and make life easier or more convenient, rather than on how they help us better glorify God. We pray mainly about our personal goals, not God's purposes. We prioritize convenience and comfort over sacrifice and obedience. And it's so easy to embrace, because even though it is straight out of the world, it has been unquestionably accepted in the culture of most families and churches. When I believe it's all about me, I will soon buy into the lie that I can change the world not just apart from community, but apart from *God*.

This idea that we can live independently from God isn't new. It's the very first lie ever told. Back in the Garden of Eden, the serpent said to Eve, "Did God really say, 'You must not eat from any tree in the garden'?" Followed by, "You will not certainly die . . . your eyes will be opened, and you will be like God" (Genesis 3:1, 4–5).

The devil's strategy from the beginning is to make us think we can be like God and thus live independently from Him. The devil wants us to shift our gaze away from God and toward ourselves and our own plans. C. S. Lewis captures this tactic masterfully in *The Screwtape Letters,* where the senior demon Screwtape writes to his nephew Wormwood, saying: "The best thing, where it is possible, is to keep the patient [that's us] from the serious intention of praying altogether . . . to turn their gaze away from Him towards themselves."[1]

Slowly, subtly, our faith becomes centered around our needs, our goals, and our comfort. We begin to treat God as a divine assistant rather than the Sovereign King. He becomes the One who blesses our dreams rather than the One who defines them.

This lie quietly shifts God from the center of the story to the margins. It recasts Him as a supporting character in our pursuit of success, rather than the Author and Perfecter of our faith.

This first lie is the one that most threatens our ability to live with unshakable faith in a secular age. It is also the most difficult one to discern. It's the hardest to recognize, because it doesn't feel wrong. It hides behind good things: self-care, ambition, even calling. It sounds like wisdom, earns applause, and slips into our prayers unnoticed—quietly shifting the focus from God to ourselves.

Unfortunately, this lie doesn't just affect what we do. Over time, it reshapes who we are. It forms a distorted identity—one that leads to spiritual disconnection and a faith that can't endure life's storms.

THE COUNTERFEIT IDENTITY: THE SELF-CENTERED WORSHIPER

The enemy's goal isn't just to tempt us into sin—it's to reshape our identity by distorting our worship. Worship determines what—or who—is at the center of our lives. When the center shifts from God to self, everything else begins to unravel.

While the lie that it's all about me may not lead to open rebellion, it does something far more dangerous: It leads to subtle redefinition. We may still believe in God. We may still sing the songs. But slowly, we begin to believe that the purpose of faith is to serve our dreams, our goals, and our fulfillment. Our worship then becomes compromised as the object of our worship has quietly changed.

And that's how a counterfeit identity is formed.

A counterfeit identity is a version of the self shaped more by cultural values and personal desires than by God's truth. It may still use spiritual language. It may even look impressive on the outside. But it's no longer rooted in surrender. It tells us that our value comes from what we accomplish, how we feel, or how others see us. It reframes "you were made for a purpose" into "your purpose is your personal fulfillment."

The enemy's goal isn't just to tempt us into sin—it's to reshape our identity by distorting our worship.

Over time this inevitably leads to more anxiety, isolation, and insecurity. We strive endlessly for meaning, but never find rest. We chase fulfillment on our terms, but end up malnourished spiritually, mentally, and emotionally. In trying to create ourselves, we disconnect from the One who made us—and that disconnection hinders true flourishing.

The danger is not just spiritual—it's personal and relational. Modern research paints a sobering picture:

- One study found that loneliness shortens a person's life by fifteen years—the equivalent impact of smoking fifteen cigarettes a day.[2]
- According to *Harvard Magazine,* 61 percent of Americans report feeling lonely.[3]
- Young adults are the most affected. Gen Z scores the

highest for loneliness, despite being the most digitally connected generation.[4]
- Former U.S. Surgeon General Vivek Murthy has declared loneliness a national epidemic, stating, "Social connection is a fundamental human need, as essential to survival as food, water, and shelter."[5]

These findings confirm what Scripture has long told us: When we center life around self we lose the very connection our souls were made for. A counterfeit identity doesn't just fall short—it erodes our joy, community, and well-being.

This identity shift rarely happens all at once. It's slow. Subtle. It doesn't usually begin with a rejection of God—it begins with a redefinition of His role. We may still go through the motions. We may still show up to church. But internally, something has shifted. We've replaced God as the center of our story and put ourselves there instead.

This is how the enemy gains ground—not by turning us away from faith, but by reshaping it around us. By turning God into a means to an end, rather than the end Himself. And once that lie takes root, everything starts to change. Our prayers become more about control than communion. Our worship becomes a performance instead of a posture. And without realizing it, we've traded a true identity for a counterfeit one.

That's how the Self-Centered Worshiper is formed—not through rebellion but through quiet drift.

True worship begins with surrender. It puts God at the center. It's rooted in awe, not entitlement—in reverence, not performance. But when our worship shifts from God-centered to self-centered, something subtle yet significant happens: Our identity begins to change.

Instead of seeing ourselves as beloved children of God—created in His image and called to reflect His glory—we begin to define ourselves by our achievements, our emotions, or the approval of others. We carry the weight of self-justification and image management. The result is exhaustion and insecurity.

But when God is at the center, our identity is no longer something we have to earn or curate. It is something we receive. We live not *for* validation but *from* it. This shift allows us to live with humility and confidence, knowing that our worth is anchored in something unshakable: the love of a holy God who has called us His own.

The Self-Centered Worshiper still believes in God, but primarily in a God who exists to serve their needs. They pray, but mainly when something's wrong. They worship, but only when the music or message stirs their emotions. Their view of God is functional, not relational.

God has become a part of their life, rather than the center of it.

I've experienced the destructive nature of this lie more times than I can count. When I'm feeling overwhelmed by responsibilities, or when things aren't going my way, I can start treating prayer as a way to control outcomes rather than surrender to God's will. I'll still show up. I may even be leading others. But underneath, I'm operating as if God exists to support my agenda—not the other way around. I'm doing ministry *for* Him instead of *with* Him—and under His authority.

And here's the tricky part: It's entirely possible to adopt this identity and still look very spiritual on the outside. You might still be serving others. Still posting Scripture on social media. Still leading a small group. But underneath all that activity is a subtle shift: God has become a means to an end. And that end, more often than not, is *you*—your reputation, your fulfillment, your influence.

Even so, Scripture and experience tell us that when we put ourselves at the center of the story, we end up with shallow roots. We may see quick fruit. We may even gain followers or influence. But our souls become dry, our passion becomes unsustainable, and our faith becomes fragile, built on the shifting sand of self rather than the Rock.

This self-centered identity, once normalized, becomes a filter for everything. Worship is measured by how it makes *me* feel. Church is evaluated by whether *my* needs are met. Obedience becomes optional if it interferes with *my* plan. Even our view of justice or service gets co-opted by the pursuit of personal fulfillment, rather than Spirit-led sacrifice.

But here's the good news: God is inviting us to something deeper and better. His kindness leads us to repentance. He gently but firmly calls us back to the place where worship is more about *who He is* than what we can get from Him.

When we recenter our lives around Jesus—not just as Savior, but as Lord—everything changes. Our dreams get refined. Our motives are purified. Our worship becomes vibrant. And we begin to live with a freedom and power that doesn't come from chasing our own greatness, but from surrendering to His.

Self-centered worship hides behind a mask of piety. It may look composed—even reverent—but underneath it's driven by pride, self-importance, and control. It approaches God with an unspoken demand to be seen, affirmed, or rewarded.

But God-centered worship has a totally different posture. We come with open hands and humble hearts. We kneel in reverence. We lift our hands in surrender. We open ourselves to receive.

RE-CENTERING OUR WORSHIP

Who—or what—we worship shapes everything. If the enemy can distort our worship, he can distort our identity, our desires, and ultimately, our lives.

This is why idolatry is one of the most dominant themes in the Old Testament. Because at its core, idolatry is false worship—giving our primary affection to something other than God. And today, it rarely looks like golden calves or carved images. More often, it looks like elevating good things to *ultimate* things: success, family, reputation, freedom.

When we believe the lie that "it's all about me," idolatry takes root even in a Christian's life. When God is no longer at the center, something else always fills that space. And most often, that "something" is us. We become the object of our own worship.

But this pattern isn't new. It's ancient. That's why the very first of the Ten Commandments is this: "You shall have no other gods before me" (Exodus 20:3). We were made to worship. The question isn't *if* we will worship—it's *who* we will worship. Repeatedly, Israel forgot this. They turned to the idols of surrounding nations. And each time, God raised up prophets to call them back—not just from false religion, but from misplaced worship. Because when our view of God is diminished, we naturally elevate something else—and more often than not, that's ourselves.

Who—or what—we worship shapes everything.

This is exactly what we see in our cultural moment today with expressive individualism—the belief that the highest purpose in life is to discover, define, and express your own identity. In this worldview, the self is sacred. The path to wholeness is found not in surrender to God, but in asserting your truth, pursuing your desires, and being affirmed for who you feel yourself to be.

We can see this influence most clearly in how some churches talk about sin. Instead of naming it as rebellion against a holy God, they reframe sin as a "mistake" or "unhealthy decision." Influenced by this cultural moment, sermons start to prioritize self-esteem over surrender, and affirmation over transformation. Conviction is softened. Repentance is optional. The gospel becomes a tool for personal growth, not a call to die to self and follow Jesus.

Now, let's be clear: God created each of us uniquely. Personal growth, creativity, and authenticity reflect His image when they're rightly ordered. The danger is not in expressing who we are, but in defining ourselves apart from God. The problem arises when self-expression replaces God's authority and becomes our highest aim.

There's a kind of self-expression that flows from intimacy with God—a musician writing songs that give voice to both pain and hope, or a teacher using her voice to encourage others and serve with integrity. These expressions reflect the image of a Creator who made us with purpose. But there's also a kind of self-expression that cuts God out of the picture entirely. It says, "This is who I am—take it or leave it," and demands affirmation from others to feel whole. Instead of glorifying God, it places the self at the center and asks others to orbit around it.

We see this especially in progressive Christianity, where one of the greatest fears is *excluding* someone. That fear often comes from a sincere desire to reflect God's love. But when inclusion is elevated above repentance, and grace is divorced from holiness, the gospel gets hollowed out. Our greatest problem isn't exclusion from one another—it's separation from God. And that separation can only be healed through repentance and faith in Jesus.

It all comes back to how we see ourselves—and who we worship. What is our starting point? Are we essentially good people in need of affirmation? Or are we broken sinners in need of redemption?

A biblical worldview starts with God, not us. It removes us from the center of the story. And that re-centering is itself an act of worship and repentance. It's a reversal of the original error of Adam and Eve, which is to reach for God's throne and make ourselves the focus.

Repentance begins by acknowledging, "I am not God. He is. I am not the center. He is." And when that truth takes root, worship begins to flow—not as an emotional reaction, but as a right and natural response.

As Psalm 130:3 says, "If you, LORD, kept a record of sins, Lord, who could stand?" None of us deserves to be in God's presence. Yet because of Jesus, we're invited in.

That's what makes worship so powerful. It's not just singing songs. It's realigning our hearts with reality. And reality is this: There is one God, and we are not Him.

And that's not bad news—it's the best news. Because if we were at the center, everything would rise and fall on our strength, our wisdom, our ability to hold it all together. But it doesn't. God is God—and He is good, sovereign, just, and merciful. He invites us to surrender not to lose ourselves, but to find life in Him.

THE TRUTH: IT STARTS WITH GOD

This truth reorients everything: Life isn't about finding yourself—it's about returning to God.

The lie says, "It's all about me."

But the truth is, it all starts—and ends—with Him.

This better way recognizes we were made to revolve around His glory. To live into His story.

He's not waiting for you to perform or prove your worth. He's inviting you to come back to the true center—His presence and His truth.

This is the clarity we need in a culture of confusion: God is not on the edges. He is at the center. And in His mercy, He draws near—not to affirm our self-centered ways, but to rescue us from them.

From the Garden of Eden to the tabernacle in the wilderness, from the manger in Bethlehem to the Spirit dwelling within us today, God has always been drawing near to His people. Not because we deserve it, but because He desires intimacy with us. He comes near to call us back to Himself.

Jesus' first public message made that clear: "Repent, for the kingdom of heaven has come near" (Matthew 4:17). The kingdom drew near not because we found God, but because God came to find us. He stepped into our story to re-center it around Himself.

The apostle Paul echoed this truth in Athens: "God did this so that they would seek him and perhaps reach out for him and find him, though he is not far from any one of us" (Acts 17:27). He is near—not to orbit our lives, but to invite us into His.

But His nearness demands a response. The presence of a

holy God calls us to more than inspiration—it calls us to repentance. Worship begins when we step off the throne and see Jesus already seated there.

> *Since we are receiving a Kingdom that is unshakable, let us be thankful and please God by worshiping him with holy fear and awe.*
>
> —*Hebrews 12:28* (NLT)

Scripture shows us that holiness is both a gift and a demand. God is the one who makes us holy—that's the gift. But He also calls us to live in holiness—that's the demand.

His holiness draws us in, but it also calls us higher. It's like opposite poles of a magnet working together: there's a pull and a push. *Come close . . . but take off your sandals.* Think of Moses before the burning bush—invited into God's presence, yet reminded of God's majesty.[6] That's the paradox of holiness: It welcomes us with intimacy but confronts us with reverence.

And this is good for us. God's holiness is like the love of a parent—both tender and demanding. A loving parent doesn't affirm everything a child does; they guide, correct, and call their child to maturity. In the same way, holiness refuses to leave us as we are. It pulls us out of complacency. It lifts our vision. It shapes us into who we were created to be—not by shaming us, but by drawing us into something better.

True worship holds both truths at once: God is near, and God is holy. That's what reshapes us. That's what pulls us out of self-centered faith and reorients us around Him.

As Psalm 145:18 says, "The Lord is near to all who call on him, to all who call on him in truth." Not to all who have it figured out. Not to all who have a perfect past. But to those who come in truth and humility.

When we come to God in truth, everything changes. Our worship becomes honest, not performative. Faith becomes integrated, not compartmentalized. Identity becomes rooted in Christ, not centered on self.

This is what it means to be a True Worshiper. Jesus said, "A time is coming and has now come when the true worshipers will worship the Father in the Spirit and in truth, for they are the kind of worshipers the Father seeks" (John 4:23).

That's the vision. Not perfect worshipers. Not impressive worshipers. But *true* ones.

People whose hearts are humbled, whose lives are surrendered, and whose gaze is fixed on the only one worthy.

And the beauty of it all? God is seeking you. He's not repelled by your past or put off by your questions, but wants to be known by you—and is drawing near to call you back to a relationship that re-centers you.

THE COMMITMENT: GOD-CENTERED WORSHIP (TRUE WORSHIP)

One verse that's anchored me for years is Matthew 6:33: "Seek first the kingdom of God and His righteousness, and all these things shall be added to you" (NKJV). It's a simple but powerful reminder: When God is at the center, everything else finds its place. I've come back to that truth again and again—in leadership, in parenting, in finances, and especially in seasons of uncertainty.

That's the heart of a True Worshiper: the humble confession, "I am not the center of the story—Jesus is." As Paul wrote, "Offer your bodies as a living sacrifice, holy and pleasing to God—this is your true and proper worship" (Romans 12:1). True worship begins with repentance and leads to renewal. It's not about perfect appearances or polished performances. It's about bringing your whole heart to God—especially the parts you've been tempted to keep to yourself.

Do you believe that a life of repentance and worship leads to renewal? That refusing to worship anything other than God brings a deeper kind of wholeness? I am not suggesting that true worship will make you wealthy. But I am saying it will satisfy you in a way nothing else can. Because true worship connects your heart to the heart of your Creator.

This is why I love worshiping alongside those who are just beginning their journey—people in recovery, people off the streets, people who've hit bottom and found grace. There's a rawness and a desperation in their worship that reminds me of what God is really after: a surrendered heart.

Because when you give God everything, worship stops being something you just do at church—it becomes a way of life. A rhythm. A posture of the soul.

You begin to see all of life as sacred. Work becomes worship, as you trust God in both your effort and your outcomes. Rest becomes worship, as you remember He is God and you are not. Your decisions, your relationships, your finances, your time—they all become daily offerings laid before the One who is worthy.

Even your morning routines shift. Instead of starting your day by processing your stresses, you start by asking: "God, what's on Your heart today?"

And as that shift happens, you begin to find what you've

been searching for all along, not in self-promotion or self-fulfillment, but in self-surrender: the peace, joy, and purpose that come only through the abiding presence of God.

That's what it means to resist the lie and embrace the truth. To move from being a Self-Centered Worshiper to becoming a True Worshiper.

WALKING IT OUT

For many years, our church has begun the new year with twenty-one days of prayer and fasting. Every January, hundreds of people wake up early to pray and worship together on Zoom. We fast from meals or media, not as a ritual, but as a way of clearing space. Making room for God at the center again. It's not just a spiritual reset. It's a re-centering of the heart.

People often begin those twenty-one days weary—burned out from the holidays, burdened by their goals. But slowly, as they worship, something shifts. Schedules change. Screens fade. And surrender begins. That's the power of corporate worship. It reminds us we're not the point. God is.

And when your life becomes centered around worship, it begins to overflow. You don't have to manufacture passion or chase meaning. You simply live in rhythm with the One you were made for—and others notice.

Worship also becomes personal. One practice that's helped anchor me is the ACTS prayer framework: Adoration, Confession, Thanksgiving, and Supplication. It's not complicated, but praying in that order reorients me. It helps me begin not with my needs, but with God's greatness.

Another practice? Simply showing up for worship—even when I don't feel like it. Especially when I'm not leading or serving. There's something powerful about singing with the people of God, even on the days we feel dry. That act of showing up reminds me I'm not alone. And reminds me of what's true.

Worship doesn't need a stage. It doesn't even need a song. It just needs a surrendered heart. You don't have to be a pastor or a musician to be a True Worshiper. You just have to give God what's already His—your attention, your affection, your life.

So start simple. Show up. Sing loud. Confess honestly. Kneel in prayer when you rise or before you sleep. Lift your hands when you pray. But most of all, surrender. Let your worship be love, not performance.

And when you do, you'll discover something beautiful: Your life will become a song that others can hear—even when no music is playing.

THE DEPTH GOD DESIRES

This will require you to understand the difference between vulnerability and repentance. We are living in a cultural moment where we've mistaken vulnerability for repentance.

Vulnerability says, "Here's what I'm going through."

Repentance says, "Here's what I'm turning from."

Vulnerability keeps it real.

Repentance keeps it real by confessing sin and turning back to God.

If there's no true repentance, then we're simply managing sin, not crucifying it.

This is exactly what the enemy wants. As Screwtape says to his junior devil: "As long as he retains externally the habits of a

Christian he can still be made to think of himself as one . . . And while he thinks that, we do not have to contend with the explicit repentance of a definite, fully recognized, sin, but only with his vague, though uneasy, feeling that he hasn't been doing very well lately."[7]

True revival always begins with repentance.

What started as an ordinary Wednesday morning chapel service at Asbury University in Wilmore, Kentucky, quickly became something no one could have expected. Without any famous speakers or promotion, students lingered in prayer and worship—and they never really stopped. What followed was a multi-week, Spirit-led gathering filled with prayer, repentance, and lives being surrendered to Jesus.

Word of what was happening spread quickly. Soon students from other colleges began arriving, drawn by the hunger and holiness of what God was doing. In the days that followed, people came from across the country—and even from as far as Russia and Japan. Media outlets showed up to cover the story, but the real headline was this: Lives were being changed. Furthermore, it was a movement marked not by hype, but by humility.[8]

And what marked that hunger? A shift in center. Jesus wasn't just included—He was enthroned.

We felt the ripple effect of that revival in our own church in Washington, D.C. Recent Asbury graduates, visiting students, and others who had experienced the outpouring brought a renewed hunger for God with them.

There was no big stage, no celebrity preacher, no LED wall. Just prayer, worship, and repentance—with Jesus at the center.

I watched as the same hunger began to grow in our community. Students lingered after services. People confessed sin more freely in their small groups. The focus wasn't on better programs or better platforms, but on God Himself.

Because when Jesus is at the center, everything changes.

True revival always begins with repentance.

And that's the heart of this chapter: True worship displaces the lie at the heart of self-centered faith and replaces it with the truth: It's all about Him.

So, here's the invitation: Don't settle for a version of Christianity that leaves you unchanged. Don't embrace a faith that asks nothing of you. Don't reduce worship to your preferences.

Instead, let your life be marked by full surrender. Let repentance become your rhythm. Let worship reshape your identity.

Don't be content to admire Jesus—follow Him.

Now more than ever, we need True Worshipers. People who carry the fire of God's presence into a culture that's drifting from the truth. People who fear God more than man. People who will speak with grace and live with boldness.

Yes, you were born to change the world—but not in your own strength, and not for your own glory.

You were born to worship the one true God.

Start there, and everything else will follow.

But know that this kind of faith doesn't grow in isolation—it flourishes in community. That's why the next lie we must confront is this: "Church is optional."

DISCUSSION AND REFLECTION QUESTIONS

Lie 1: It's All About Me

1. **Reflecting on the Lie**

   Why do you think the lie "It's all about me" is so pervasive in today's culture? In what ways have you seen this mindset show up in your own life or in the lives of those around you?

2. **Self-Centered Worship**

   How does the "It's all about me" mindset affect the way we approach worship and prayer? In contrast, what does it look like to come before God with a posture of surrender and awe?

3. **The Enemy's Strategy**

   How does the enemy use this lie (it's all about me) to draw us away from intimacy with God? What signs might indicate that we're slipping into this mindset, even subtly?

4. **Counterfeit Identity vs. True Identity**

   How has your understanding of your identity in Christ grown or changed over time? What helps you resist the pull toward self-centered definitions of identity?

5. **Scriptural Truths About God's Nearness**

   Several scriptures affirm that God is near (e.g., Joshua 1:9, Psalm 23:4, Isaiah 41:10). Which one speaks most to you right now, and why? How can these truths help realign your worship and identity?

6. **Importance of Repentance**

   Why is repentance so essential in resisting the lie that "it's all about me"? Can you share a time when repentance deepened your relationship with God or brought freedom?

7. **Vulnerability vs. Repentance**

    What's the difference between being vulnerable and truly repenting? Why is it important that our confession leads to transformation—not just emotional honesty?

8. **Identifying Modern Idols**

    What are some common idols today that can subtly take God's place in our hearts (e.g., success, approval, comfort)? How can we regularly examine and guard our hearts from misplaced worship?

9. **Practical Steps to True Worship**

    What are some intentional ways you can cultivate a lifestyle of true worship—one that places God at the center? What spiritual practices help keep your heart aligned?

10. **Living Out the Truth**

    How can you live out the truth that God is near in your everyday life—in your relationships, work, and witness? What would it look like to live with greater awareness of His presence?

2

WHEN CHURCH FEELS OPTIONAL

From Church Shopping to Deep Community

> Surely you know that if a man can't be cured of churchgoing, the next best thing is to send him all over the neighborhood looking for the church that "suits" him until he becomes a taster or connoisseur of churches . . . The search for a "suitable" church makes the man a critic where the Enemy wants him to be a pupil.
>
> —*The Screwtape Letters,* Letter 16

In the spring of 2010, we started our church with one simple rule:

You couldn't come if you were already a part of another church.

That might sound dramatic, but we weren't interested in playing the church-swap game. We were not interested in reaching the already found. We wanted to create a church of unchurched people rather than grow by church transfer.

What we discovered was sobering. Many of the people who came had grown up in Christian homes but were no longer actively practicing their faith. Some had experienced church hurt. Others had grown disillusioned by scandals or leadership hypocrisy. Still others simply couldn't find a church that felt like home. Most were going through a season of deconstruction, wrestling with questions about race, sexuality, inequality, politics, and the church's role in society.

Deconstruction is the process of reexamining one's faith, which can lead either to deeper discipleship or to walking away from Jesus, depending on what foundation you build on.

Church shopping will lead to spiritual isolation.

It's common for those in their twenties.

You're off on your own in the real world for the first time. You're working a full-time job and trying to figure out how to do life. You're faced with tough decisions, deciding how to integrate childhood faith with the complex realities of adulthood. You're likely wrestling with questions of identity, justice, power, and how the church stewards its influence and resources.

The enemy loves this season.

It's prime time for him to sow lies and get you to deny your faith.

Let me make the premise of this chapter clear: If you do not commit to a church with a real discipleship culture, then the secular worldview will take root. It's just a matter of time. Over time, without biblical community, even the strongest convictions can start to unravel. To prevent this, you must develop a clear biblical conviction for how to be *in* but not *of* the world.

Many of us were raised in environments that emphasized how to avoid being "of" the world. We were taught to steer clear of moral compromise, to hold fast to our convictions, and to stand apart from cultural norms that oppose God's truth.

And now, here we are—*in* the world. Perhaps you are in

college or have stepped into positions of responsibility and influence. Whether you're working in education, business, healthcare, public service, technology, or the arts, you're making decisions that affect real people and real problems—issues like poverty, injustice, war, and the flourishing of communities you are part of.

But what many of us weren't prepared for is how to faithfully follow Jesus while occupying these spaces of influence. How do we resist being shaped by the very systems we're trying to redeem? How do we stay grounded in Christ when our success, reputation, or even our paycheck is tied to going with the cultural flow?

What does it look like to practice our faith in this new Babylon? How do we maintain a distinct Christian witness and practice spiritual disciplines amid a godless culture that relentlessly wants us to water down our faith?

It's in vulnerable seasons like this that the enemy whispers a dangerous lie—one that's become increasingly accepted: Church is optional.

THE LIE: CHURCH IS OPTIONAL

In their book *The Great Dechurching,* authors Jim Davis and Michael Graham highlight a significant shift in American religious participation: "More people have left the church in the last twenty-five years than all the new people who became Christians from the First Great Awakening, Second Great Awakening, and Billy Graham crusades *combined.*"[1]

This trend marks an eighty-year low in church attendance, with most Americans not attending church at all.[2] The authors also note that for the first time in eight decades of Gallup tracking, more adults in the United States don't attend church than do.[3] These findings underscore a profound transformation in the American religious landscape, with millions disengaging from traditional church participation.

Why are people leaving? Let me introduce you to Sarah. She's twenty-nine, works as an elementary school teacher, and grew up attending church every Sunday with her family. When Sarah moved to the city after college, she tried to find a church but struggled to feel at home. She bounced between congregations, finding flaws in each one: "The music is too showy here . . . The sermon feels shallow there . . . They're too political at this one." Eventually, she stopped going altogether.

"I didn't feel like I needed it anymore," Sarah confessed. "I'm still a Christian. I still pray and read my Bible. But I just couldn't deal with the drama of finding a church."

Sarah's story is not unique. Whether it's frustration with church politics, burnout from past experiences, or simply the allure of convenience (hello, Sunday morning brunch), the enemy uses subtle lies to isolate us.

Why are so many walking away? Here is what the data shows:

1. **Church Hurt**—Scandals and hypocrisy, including abuse by leaders and moral failure, are among the top reasons people lose faith. A recent Barna survey found: Two of the top sources of doubt for most people are "negative past experiences with a religious institution" and the "hypocrisy of religious people."[4] When trust is broken, it's hard to see the church as a safe space.
2. **Theological Differences**—Disagreement with church doctrine and cultural issues is one of the leading reasons people walk away. According to a 2023 PRRI survey, 56 percent of those who switched religious traditions said they

stopped believing in their religion's teachings, and 30 percent cited negative teachings about or treatment of LGBTQ people as their reason. An additional 17 percent mentioned frustration with their church's political focus. All of this reflects a growing tension between personal convictions and institutional beliefs.[5]

3. **Convenience and Drift**—Many simply drift away, not because of doctrine or scandal, but due to life patterns and the ease of opting out. A Pew survey found that 44 percent of self-identified Christians don't regularly attend church because they "practice their faith in other ways," and 28 percent say they haven't found a church they like.[6] Jim Davis and Michael Graham pointed out that much of the decline comes from people stopping attendance not out of anger or disagreement, but simply because they drifted.[7]

Given all this, it's no surprise many start to wonder, *Does church even matter anymore?*

For some, that question isn't just cultural—it's personal. The pain runs deep.

If you've been hurt by the church, I want to acknowledge your pain. Maybe you experienced judgment when you needed grace. Maybe your questions were dismissed instead of welcomed. Or perhaps you felt betrayed by someone you trusted. Whatever your story, as a pastor I want to say I'm sorry.

The failures of individuals don't negate the beauty of God's design for His church. Healing often comes through the very community we're tempted to avoid. Healing comes through leaning into a God-designed community, not running away from it.

Maybe you were told how important it was to stay strong in your faith when you went off to college. But now that you've graduated, the harder test might be right in front of you: Will you stay connected to Christian community when no one is checking in? Will you pursue the church not because you have to, but because you believe you need it?

Our church was planted at this inflection point in young adults' lives when they must decide whether to practice their faith for themselves, apart from their parents.

Perhaps at this juncture, you're no longer living in a dorm with people with the same schedule. You no longer have a built-in community through a campus ministry with people in the same stage of life.

For the first time, you must have the strength to get up, get dressed, and go alone.

It is at this moment that the enemy develops a very predictable pattern to spiritually isolate people:

He mixes the truth with a lie.

The enemy presents you with something that is true and compelling and tailored to the season. Something like "I don't need to be committed to a church to enter into a relationship with God." Which is reassuring in a difficult season when you can go straight to the Father through Jesus Christ in prayer. It's theologically true and convenient.

But once you agree with this truth, the conditions are set for a routine change to your spiritual practices. "I'm super busy so I can back off in my engagement, because God still loves me. It's not my church attendance or my Bible app performance that saves me." And this is all true.

Here is the pattern. Once your routine has changed and your guard has been let down, it's at that moment the enemy inserts a lie.

The truth is that you can *enter* a relationship with God without stepping foot inside a church. But the lie is that you can *grow* in your relationship with God apart from the church. Notice the subtlety. This belief is what then justifies the lie that church is optional.

Once you have agreed with this lie, the conditions are set for it to take root. And the lie always takes root in the form of a counterfeit identity.

COUNTERFEIT IDENTITY: THE CHURCH SHOPPER

The false identity is to become a Church Shopper.

When church is optional, I can just keep church shopping until the right one comes along. This is not difficult to do because there are so many options. We no longer live in the day of the parish model of church where you just went to the closest church to where you live. Now most people drive by dozens of churches each Sunday to arrive at the church of their choice.

When you move to a new place and begin church shopping, you usually have two overarching options:

1. Established mainline churches with nice buildings, which are usually liberal theologically and have an aging membership.
2. Evangelical churches in portable spaces that are reaching young people, but seem out of touch with the cultural issues you read about and experienced in college.

The mainline church feels boring and the evangelical church feels out of touch. Unless you have friends inviting you to one of them, you are not likely to commit.

You also don't know how long you are going to be living where you are. You are not sure you want to spend the energy building new relationships with a community you might soon leave. Having the motivation to get up, get dressed, and go alone is not a one-time thing. It persists for years to come. In a culture where marriage is being deferred until later and later in life, and many roommates rarely share your faith, it requires considerable self-discipline to continually invest in a local church community when you are always going alone.

There are plenty of sociological reasons I could share about why people become chronic Church Shoppers, but the main purpose of this chapter is to explain the *spiritual* reasons.

The senior devil Screwtape tells Wormwood, "The search for a 'suitable' church makes the man a critic where the Enemy wants him to be a pupil."[8]

God wants us to be pupils instead of critics. To be teachable. Hungry to learn and to grow as disciples. Which requires humility.

We must remember that the gospel is true even in a difficult season of searching for a church.

It is easy to forget what a blessing it is to even have the opportunity to be a Church Shopper. To have options. Millions of Christians across the globe do not have this luxury—they're limited to attending the one church in their area.[9] Yet their faith is growing stronger by the day.

The New Testament word for church is *ekklésia*—a Greek word meaning "the assembly" or "the called-out ones."[10] It never refers to a building or a broadcast. It refers to a people gathered for a purpose. In Scripture, the church is not just a collection of individual believers, each doing their own thing. It's a body, a household of faith, a family—something only fully realized when believers come together in worship, fellowship, and mission. From Pentecost onward, the church was a visible, embodied community. They didn't just believe privately; they gathered publicly. That's because Christianity was never meant to be lived in isolation. The call to follow Jesus is also a call to belong to His people.

God never designed us to live autonomously apart from His body. This is why church isn't just about avoiding isolation—it's about discovering purpose. It's the place where we grow into who we were created to be. Where our gifts are discovered. Where spiritual friendships take root. And where ordinary people are shaped into world changers through daily acts of worship, service, and love.

When Jesus calls disciples, He always places them in community.

THE CALL TO COMMUNITY

CrossFit has become one of the most popular workouts today.

It has also become one of the most expensive gyms to join. This is despite there being very little equipment, and the fact that the daily workouts are posted online each day for anyone to read. CrossFit is actually pretty straightforward to do at home for free.

So why do so many people pay so much to join CrossFit gyms?

The secret isn't in the routine or the facility. It's the community. CrossFit has cracked the code of community. There's a strong, shared bond that forms when you do something difficult with others. This is why people pay hundreds of dollars a month to join a gym with basically no equipment.

In the same way, people don't commit to a church just because of great preaching or perfect programs—they stay because it becomes a spiritual home. It's where we find encouragement when we're struggling, correction when we drift, and joy when we grow. The church is the place where we practice being the family of God together, not just for ourselves but for the sake of the world.

And it's not just spiritually true—it's backed by real-world evidence.

Ryan Burge, a leading researcher on religious trends, notes, "There is overwhelming empirical support for the value of being at a house of worship on a regular basis on all kinds of metrics: mental health, physical health, having more friends, being less lonely."[11]

Pew Research findings confirm that actively religious people report greater happiness, stronger relationships, and lower rates of depression and disease.[12] Harvard studies show that regular church attendance is linked to a significantly longer life expectancy—thanks to the deep, life-giving bonds found in spiritual community.[13]

God's design for the church isn't just about avoiding isolation. It's about discovering life as it was meant to be lived—in Him, and with His people.

The local church is where God forms us into people who look more like Jesus.

Yet even with all these benefits—spiritual, relational, even physical—there's still a pull toward isolation. That's why the enemy's strategy is so effective: It doesn't feel dangerous at first.

The reality is, you *can* enter into a relationship with Jesus *without* being a member of the church.

In the same way, you can engage with God individually—reading Scripture, praying, even worshiping on your own. But the question is, how consistent will you be over the long term without a community around you?

Here's what is at stake if you bow out of church:

- **Spiritual drift.** Without regular worship, teaching, and communion with others, our hearts inevitably grow cold.
- **Distorted identity.** Alone, it's easy to forget who you are and what you're for. You lose the mirror of godly community.
- **Shallow roots.** We trade a life of depth for a life of preference—constantly chasing a more convenient option, never fully known, never fully formed.

Something powerful happens when people from such different backgrounds come together under the lordship of Christ. When we worship and fellowship with people we would probably never choose to hang out with apart from our faith.

This is why Paul was in awe to see Jews and Gentiles worshiping together in the early church. "There is neither Jew nor Greek, there is neither slave nor free, nor is there male and female, for you are all one in Christ Jesus" (Galatians 3:28). What we have in common in Christ must be greater than what divides us in the world.

The local church is where God forms us into people who look more like Jesus—not because everyone around us is the same, but precisely because they're not.

When you commit to a local church, here's what you gain:

- **You gain perspective.** Being part of a diverse church puts you shoulder to shoulder with people whose backgrounds, stories, and spiritual gifts differ from yours.

- **You gain formation.** You're shaped not just by sermons, but by serving. By showing up for others. By letting people show up for you.
- **You gain accountability.** When you start to drift, someone notices. Someone reaches out. You're not invisible.
- **You gain covering.** In a world full of spiritual warfare, a healthy church doesn't just inspire you—it shields you.
- **You gain purpose.** You realize that your gifts aren't just for your career or your own gain—they're for building up the body. And that changes everything.

Participation in the local church is not optional.[14] The church is God's design for how He forms us as His people to become a countercultural witness for a lost world.

Most Christians say they value church community—and as humans, we're wired for it. We long to belong, even if we don't always act on it. That's why spiritual isolation doesn't usually happen in a moment—it happens slowly, subtly, over time.

I think of Marcus, a recent grad who jumped into church life right away. He was serving, was in a group, was all in. But his work and travel picked up and he started missing most Sundays. Then his small group felt like too much. Before long, he wasn't showing up at all. I saw him a couple of years later and he told me, "I didn't mean to leave—I just kind of drifted." That's often how it happens. No dramatic exit, just quiet disengagement until you're far from where you started.

The same thing that happens when I'm floating on my boogie board in the ocean happens with our spiritual lives if we are not anchored. This is the enemy's strategy, to get you to drift. He will do so by isolating you so gradually that you won't even realize it is happening.

He'll begin with your thoughts. You'll start believing and thinking things about yourself or about God that are simply not true.

This is why it is so important to spiritually discern the difference between doubt, deconstruction, and denial.

DOUBT, DECONSTRUCTION, AND DENIAL

To *doubt* means to lack confidence or be unsure of what you believe.

To doubt is part of what it means to be human. The father of the demon-possessed child confessed to Jesus upon the invitation to receive his healing, "I do believe; help me overcome my unbelief!" (Mark 9:24).

We all need to listen to, love, and care for those who doubt. As Jude says, we should "be merciful to those who doubt" (Jude v. 22).

But the problem is, some Christian spaces have turned doubt into a virtue—something to be celebrated, even emulated. Prominent voices like Rob Bell, Brian McLaren, and Richard Rohr, podcasts such as *The Liturgists,* and church networks like Blue Ocean Faith have created platforms where doubt is not only welcomed but often commended—portrayed as a hallmark of spiritual maturity rather than a step toward deeper faith.

A healthy Christian community should always create space for people to be vulnerable and process their biggest questions. People should not feel like they have to check their big questions at the doors of the church. Our biggest questions are often what can strengthen our faith the most when they are processed well.

There are real doubts that people have about faith and about church that we need to learn how to engage. Jesus listened to the doubts of Peter, John the Baptist, the woman at the well, Thomas, and the rest of the disciples. He loved them and didn't condemn them.

Yet we see that Jesus never met a doubt he liked. He charged Thomas to "stop doubting and believe" (John 20:27). He challenged Peter, "You of little faith . . . why did you doubt?" (Matthew 14:31).

Jesus ultimately resists doubt because He calls us to walk by faith. A healthy response to doubt invites discipleship, not detachment—where doubt is met with biblical truth, loving community, and Spirit-led conversation that refines faith rather than erodes it.

There is doubt, and then there is deconstruction.

Deconstruction is a step beyond doubt.

It is the process of dismantling one's accepted beliefs.

When done in the context of biblical community, deconstruction can be redemptive. Healthy deconstruction dismantles bad theology, abuse, or spiritual manipulation and helps people rediscover the truth about Christ and His Word.

That's exactly what happened for one woman in our church. She'd spent years in a community where asking questions was seen as rebellion and women weren't allowed to lead. Her love for Jesus was real, but she carried deep hurt and confusion about her place in the church.

At first, she kept her distance—suspicious, guarded, unsure if this place would be any different. But over time, through Scripture, trusted relationships, and a safe small group, she began to dismantle the faulty theology she had absorbed.

She didn't walk away from the gospel—she rediscovered it. Today, she's helping others do the same, leading with confidence and clarity.

That's what healthy deconstruction looks like—not walking away from faith, but rebuilding it more firmly on Christ.

But not every story goes that way.

Deconstruction can also become a smokescreen for something else—a way to avoid hard truths or justify choices we already want to make. If you're in that place, you need to be honest: Is your goal to grow closer to Jesus? Or are you looking for reasons to walk away?

Some people simply want to sin and not feel guilty about it. Sometimes, beneath our theological questions, there are deeper desires we haven't fully examined. We want to follow God, but we also want freedom on our own terms. If we're not careful, we can start looking for teaching that affirms what we already want to do.

Here's how that often plays out: Someone says, "I believe in the whole counsel of God"—but then starts sleeping with his girlfriend. Rather than face conviction, he googles, "Is sleeping with my girlfriend wrong as a Christian?" Inevitably, he finds a blog deconstructing purity culture, criticizing how it harmed people growing up in the church. Rather than examining that argument in light of Scripture—which he once claimed had authority in his life—he embraces a softer gospel that accommodates his choices. He'll find a church that stays quiet on the issue. Or even one that celebrates it.

Peter said, "Be alert and of sober mind. Your enemy the devil prowls around like a roaring lion looking for someone to devour" (1 Peter 5:8).

Deconstruction can be dangerous if done in isolation. Without wise counsel, it can lead you away from God rather than back to Him. That's why it matters where you go for guidance. Don't rely on social media feeds—turn to a godly community that loves you and is grounded in the Word.

Jude says, "Be merciful to those who doubt; save others by snatching them from the fire; to others show mercy, mixed with fear" (Jude 22–23).

If deconstruction goes unchecked, it can harden into denial—the point at which someone no longer wrestles with faith, but walks away from it entirely.

To *deny* means to declare something untrue, to disavow or repudiate it.

This is where Satan ultimately wants to take you, using the spirit of this age as one of his primary tools. For them, Jude says, we must "[snatch] them from the fire." This is life or death. This is beyond an indirect personal warning. This is when you invite your community group to enter a time of prayer and fasting followed by initiating an intervention meeting.

Doubt is more passive. It happens *to* you.

Denying your faith is active. You know it is happening, and you are choosing it.

This is what happened to Judas, who got to a point where he was actively resisting God. If you're not careful, this could happen to you. I have extensive experience watching people morph into heretics and even false prophets. Through my observations, I have noticed it's usually gradual. It's more about the *trajectory* of their beliefs, not just what they say in an isolated moment.

There was a young man in our church years ago who led a small group, served on Sundays, and was even discerning a call to ministry. But over time, something shifted. He began pulling back—first from community, then from daily prayer, then from leadership. It wasn't a scandal. It was a slow fade. He started sharing articles that subtly undermined core Christian doctrines. At first, it seemed like intellectual curiosity. But soon, Jesus was no longer his Savior—He was just a historical figure, one option among many.

It didn't happen overnight. It started with honest doubts, moved into unchecked deconstruction, and ended in open denial. This man still calls himself spiritual, but his faith has no anchor. The trajectory was clear, even if the change felt gradual. That's why we must stay alert—not just for ourselves, but for one another.

If you evaluate someone based on a snapshot of what they say or of one season of life, they may look like they have a historic orthodox Christian faith—they will likely insist that they do. However, if you look at their trajectory, you may see a trend toward undermining core doctrine.

Our church has a covenant that outlines lifestyle commitments expected of anyone serving in leadership. It includes things like abstaining from sex outside of marriage, avoiding abuse of drugs or alcohol, investing financially in the church, and caring for the poor. These aren't extreme—they're basic commitments for anyone seeking to follow Jesus.

I remember a leader in our church who insisted they agreed with our statement of faith and our lifestyle covenant but consistently pushed back, particularly around abstaining from sex outside of marriage. Over time, it became clear they were more energized by questioning God's clear biblical standards than by living them out. Years later, when this person was no longer in leadership and no longer involved in church, it became clear: They had been looking for theological cover to justify their desires.

If we are not careful, we will give in to the temptation to water down core beliefs in an effort to reach more people. But in doing so, Jesus will become a suggestion, not a Savior. He'll no longer be *the Way,* but merely *a way.*

And when we disconnect from biblical community, it becomes even harder to discern truth from error. False prophets don't show up with horns and pitchforks. Jesus said they come performing signs and wonders.[15] But He also said we'll know them by their fruit—and that kind of fruit is best discerned in community.[16]

Is their life integrated? Do they show humility, serve the poor, and love children? Does their faith go beyond Sunday and show up in the workplace? This kind of fruit often becomes visible only when people walk closely with others who know them well.

Many today have reduced Jesus to a good example—someone who inspires us to be more loving and inclusive. But Jesus is not just a moral teacher. He's the Son of God who alone can forgive sin and reconcile us to a holy God. And that truth is best guarded and passed on in a church that teaches and lives it faithfully.

In my experience, chronic Church Shoppers begin a journey that starts with centering doubt, then progresses to celebrating unhealthy deconstruction, and ultimately concludes by tolerating denial. This is the long-term fruit of spiritual isolation.

We must resist the secular lie of "you do you" and instead speak the truth in love. Too much is at stake to stay silent while so many of our friends and family drift away from the faith they once professed.

WHAT JESUS WANTS FROM HIS CHURCH

If you've been hurt or disappointed by the church, you're not alone. But what if, instead of walking away, you're being invited by God to help build something better? Not to ignore what's broken, but to be part of the renewal.

Because the best place to see what Jesus truly desires for His church isn't in our opinions but in His own words.

If we ever start to wonder whether the church still matters, we need only look at Jesus. In Revelation, we see Him not as a distant critic of the church, but as a High Priest walking among the lampstands (Revelation 1:13)—present, attentive, and deeply invested. He hasn't given up on His church. He is purifying it.

In His letters to the seven churches (Revelation 2–3), Jesus told us exactly what He's looking for. He longs for a church that

- **loves Him first** (*Ephesus*)—not just with correct doctrine, but with passion and intimacy.
- **stays faithful under pressure** (*Smyrna*)—even when following Him costs everything.
- **refuses compromise** (*Pergamum and Thyatira*)—standing for truth and holiness in a culture of confusion.
- **awakens from spiritual complacency** (*Sardis*)—trading appearance of life for the power of it.
- **holds fast to His Word** (*Philadelphia*)—remaining obedient even when strength is small.
- **repents of lukewarmness** (*Laodicea*)—turning back to Him with zeal when we drift.

Jesus' love for the church is fierce and unwavering. He corrects what is off, strengthens what is weak, and calls His people to rise. If the church were optional, Jesus wouldn't bother. But He does—and He's still walking among us, refining His bride for the day He returns.

THE TRUTH: THE CHURCH IS GOD'S PLAN FOR YOU

The truth is, God designed the church for a unique role.

Jesus told us that He would build His *church,* and the gates of hell will not prevail (Matthew 16:18).

Jesus used the word *ekklésia* here, a term familiar in Greek civic life to describe a public assembly. But Jesus redefined *ekklésia* to describe a people called out by God, gathered in His name, and sent with His authority to embody and advance the kingdom of heaven on earth.

From Genesis to Revelation, God is a gatherer. He gathers His people to Himself—first in the garden, then in the wilderness, later at the temple, and now in the church. God's gathering is not random or optional. It is purposeful. Through gathering, He forms, equips, corrects, and empowers His people. He gathers us for worship, for repentance, for prayer, for mission, and for witness to the world.

As my spiritual father Stuart McAlpine put it, "We don't gather for pragmatic reasons, but for Presence." We are gathered to Him, and for Him.

The church is God's instrument to advance the agenda of heaven over and against the agenda of the enemy. It is through the church—this flawed but Spirit-empowered community—that God reveals His wisdom (Ephesians 3:10), unleashes His power (Acts 1:8), and builds up His people (Ephesians 4:11–13).

When young people see church as optional, I know we have failed to communicate the power of what Jesus is teaching here.

The local church is God's plan to change the world. There is no other institution on earth like it. There is no other community that has been given spiritual authority to help form people into the likeness of Christ. The local church is the only community on earth where your deepest wounds can be healed and your truest calling can be affirmed. Where both your brokenness and your giftings are welcomed. Where the power of the Spirit is not just something we read about, but something we experience together.

The reality is that no other institution or even sector of society has spiritual formation as its bottom line. This is what makes the local church the most strategic sector of society. Because if we get this sector right, we will influence every other sector with people who have been formed in the way of Jesus. We will have godly nurses and doctors practicing the ministry of healing. We will have godly artists and athletes using their platform for Christ.

We will have godly scientists pursuing groundbreaking research for the glory of God. There will be godly lawyers, entrepreneurs, educators, and social workers. We will even have godly politicians who are truly devoted to public service rather than serving themselves.

And most important, we will have godly homes. Our marriages will be different. Our parenting will be different. The ripple effect of formation in the local church will affect every sector of society.

Thankfully you don't have to work for the church to believe it is the most strategic sector. You simply join it and engage. While your personal influence will fade, the spiritual influence of the church will endure forever.

Your job, your non-profit, your school—those are good things. God can use them powerfully. But the one thing Jesus promised to return for is His church. That's why our deepest identity and lasting impact must be rooted there.

He's coming back for His church—His bride. He's longing for one without spot or wrinkle. One who has been washed cleaned with water through the Word.[17] A people prepared in holiness, unity, and love.

I dream that one day when young people think about changing the world, the majority will see the local church as the way to do it. They'll understand the unique role of the local church in spiritually equipping and discipling people to be able to sustain lifelong kingdom influence. They'll understand that kingdom impact in each sector of society is predicated upon the character formation that happens among leaders in the local church.

God wants the gospel to touch every area of society, but the way He does that is through His gathered people. Through those who have come together across differences to worship the Lamb of God who takes away the sins of the world.[18]

We are not just a crowd. We are a covenant family. Not just a service, but a sent people. Not scattered believers, but the gathered church.

The church is God's plan for you. And for the world.

THE COMMITMENT: COMMIT TO A CHURCH (DEEP COMMUNITY)

This is an invitation to be spiritually formed through the local church.

The temptation is to keep shopping, keep scrolling, and wait for the perfect church with the perfect answers to come around.

But the church is not a building.

The church is made up of imperfect people.

There are no perfect churches because there are no perfect people, including you.

And yet, those who benefit most from the church are those

who take ownership of it. *You* are the church. What if the very thing you long to see in the church is something God wants to bring to life through *you*? It doesn't have to be perfect—it just has to start with your yes.

The burden God has put on your heart, combined with your yes, could be the start of something new. Your yes could be the beginning of a new ministry in the church, one that is not only an answer to your prayers but the prayers of many others who have the same felt need.

God is not calling you to shop for a church. He is calling you to build one.

I encourage you to reflect on this question: What is my posture toward the church?

Are you leaning in or out? If you're leaning out, why? Do you have doubts that are keeping you from engaging? Is there some real church hurt you need to work through? Or unconfessed sin you're trying to justify?

Catching a sermon clip online or brunching with believers once a month is not enough to sustain your faith. God has created you for something deeper—something richer than just consuming content and having casual acquaintances.

When you're deeply rooted in a local church, you're not just being discipled—you're creating a culture you can invite others into. It's not enough to build relationships with neighbors and co-workers and tell them you are a Christian. They will not be discipled and grow if you do not have a larger community to invite them into.

If you want to grow a robust faith in an increasingly secular age, it won't happen for you or your friends through occasional church attendance or one-off spiritual conversations. The cultural tide is moving too quickly. You are not strong enough to swim against it on your own.

You must be a committed part of a local church where you are being discipled, discipling others, and regularly surrendering every area of your life to God.

The enemy wants to spiritually isolate you. And he will use any means necessary to keep you from fellowship with others, including doubt, deconstruction, and denial. Don't allow your pride to keep you from the spiritual community God has designed you for. Don't allow your desire for the perfect church to keep you from committing to an imperfect church that worships a perfect God.

I believe God has placed a church in your local community specifically for you. Will you walk through the doors and commit?

God is not calling you to shop for a church. He is calling you to build one—with your prayers, your gifts, your presence, and your perseverance.

Because if you don't, isolation is only phase one. Once you're detached from community, the enemy's next move is to silence your witness.

DISCUSSION AND REFLECTION QUESTIONS

Lie 2: Church Is Optional

1. **Challenges of Commitment**

   What has been your experience—spiritually, emotionally, or practically—with finding and committing to a local church? What challenges have you faced in that process?

2. **Church Shopper Mentality**

   Have you ever fallen into the pattern of being a Church Shopper (or church hopper)? What motivated this behavior, and what did you learn from it?

3. **Balancing Preferences and Purpose**

   What are your nonnegotiables when looking for a church? What preferences should you let go of?

4. **Impact of Isolation**

   In what ways has spiritual isolation affected your faith?

5. **God's Plan for the Church**

   How does the idea that the church is God's plan for you challenge or affirm your current view of church involvement? What might change in your life if you really believed that?

6. **Critic vs. Pupil**

   Screwtape suggests that seeking a "suitable church" turns a person into a critic rather than a pupil. How have you seen this shift from learner to critic in your life or others'?

7. **Doubt vs. Deconstruction**

   How do you distinguish between healthy doubts about the church and unhealthy deconstruction that leads to isolation?

8. **Being in, Not of, the World**

   What does it look like for a church to form disciples who are in the world but not of it? How can you model and encourage that in your community?

9. **Post-College Transition**

   Why do you think many young adults find church optional during or after college? What steps can churches take to address this trend?

10. **Encouraging One Another**

    How can we help one another stay committed to a church community, even when it feels imperfect or inconvenient? What's one step we can take this month?

3

WHEN FAITH BECOMES PRIVATE

From Lukewarm Belief to Bold Witness

> Indeed the safest road to Hell is the gradual one—the gentle slope, soft underfoot, without sudden turnings, without milestones, without signposts.
>
> —*The Screwtape Letters,* Letter 12

It was my senior year of college. I was about to graduate from an elite private university. All my friends were celebrating their recent admissions to prestigious graduate schools or getting ready to start high-paying consulting jobs.

But I heard God say, *Give everything away. Serve Me on the streets of Boston.*

God was calling me to leave behind my comfortable, upwardly mobile life as a suburban kid to serve Him.

My friends thought I was crazy. My family thought I was crazy. It *was* crazy.

That's exactly how I knew it was the Lord.

One of the ways I know God is speaking to me is that I feel immense peace about something that would normally be way out of my comfort zone. As a type A achiever, I was way out of my comfort zone, but I could sense the weight of the Holy Spirit. God was speaking. I read the words Jesus spoke to His disciples, and I knew they weren't just for them. I knew they were for me:

> Don't take any money in your money belts—no gold, silver, or even copper coins. Don't carry a traveler's bag with a change of clothes and sandals or even a walking stick. Don't hesitate to accept hospitality, because those who work deserve to be fed. (Matthew 10:9–10, NLT)

This lie is about nominal Christianity.

God was about to disrupt the top-down version of service that I was accustomed to as a privileged kid. He was about to teach me to be dependent on strangers for my needs, which would open doors for me to share my faith. He was about to reveal to me the gift of two-way relationships of giving and receiving.

I gave away everything I had, including my nice car, and moved to Boston with nothing but a backpack.

It ended up being one of the most challenging yet rewarding experiences of my life. I soon met "Ma Siss" who was the Mother Teresa of Boston, who took me in off the streets. She gave me a place to stay and invited me to lead a Bible study in the abandoned auto repair shop she had just purchased. She had turned it into a neighborhood thrift shop, but after we met, God gave her a spiritual vision for the place.

She became the person of peace that Jesus tells us to look for when going to minister in a new area.[1] It's the idea that if an established community leader is open to you and comes to faith in Christ, there is a high chance they could lead their whole community to Christ.

Shortly after, I met my wife, Amy.

I'm not sure what Amy saw in me during that season. It

certainly wasn't my bank account! Together we began our relationship by leading this Bible study that soon grew into a new church we called Quincy Street Missional Church. Here I was, a twenty-two-year-old white boy from the suburbs of Richmond, serving as the lead pastor of a black church in inner city Boston.

It was such a bizarre story that Michael Paulson, a Pulitzer Prize–winning religion reporter from *The Boston Globe,* spent three years attending our church so that he could write a feature about my relationship with Ma Siss that would run on the front page of the *Globe* for four days.[2]

Those five years in Boston were deeply transformative. It was my school of ministry where I learned how to fully rely on God.

My suburban upbringing had made it easy to compartmentalize my faith. Everything in my world was professionally done and had its own place. You have school over here, sports there, work there, friends there, and church over there. If you have a problem in one of those areas, you can usually isolate it and treat it with minimal disruption to the rest of your life. When you have resources, it is much easier to keep going because you can hire a specialist to help treat your problem and minimize its impact on other areas of your life.

But when you are poor, you can't compartmentalize your life. One unfortunate circumstance affects every area. And it also works the other way. One positive event affects every other area.

It's one of the reasons people living on the streets are often more active in sharing their faith. They experience the spiritual benefits of not being able to compartmentalize their life. They can't do this in the natural realm, so why would they think to do this in the spiritual realm?

We grow the most spiritually when we must fully rely on God. When we can no longer compartmentalize our faith and are forced to confront whether we really believe what we claim. For me, that meant giving away everything and depending on other people to take care of me on one of the poorest streets of Boston, forcing me to depend on God in ways I never had.

The challenge we are faced with today is how pursuing a comfortable life leads to a compartmentalized life, where faith is kept to yourself.

THE LIE: FAITH IS PRIVATE

The third lie the enemy is tempting Christians to believe today is that our faith is to be private.

Private, meaning there is not a public component of my faith. It's meant only for me and one part of my life, not for everyone.

Faith is meant to be personal, meaning it must be owned and experienced at the intimate level between us and God. However, our faith was never meant to be hidden or restricted to the personal level.

Jesus said, "You are the light of the world. A town built on a hill cannot be hidden. Neither do people light a lamp and put it under a bowl. Instead they put it on its stand, and it gives light to everyone in the house. In the same way, let your light shine before others, that they may see your good deeds and glorify your Father in heaven" (Matthew 5:14–16).

Our faith is meant to be lived out loud.

This is one of the reasons Jesus made such a big deal out of baptism. And why every Christian tradition has practiced it for two thousand years. In baptism we publicly renounce sin and confess Jesus as Savior and Lord.

Baptism is fundamentally a public act. You are telling the world that you are now publicly associating yourself with Jesus.

It's like my wedding ring—when others see it, they know I am publicly announcing my association with Amy. I'm saying I am not ashamed of my marriage to her. In fact, when I go to the gym, I have one of those cheap silicon rings that I wear, to let people know while I'm getting my lift on that these muscles are taken!

Your baptism is your ring. It's the seal where you are publicly identifying yourself as a follower of Jesus.

And just like your wedding day is day one of a lifelong journey of marriage, your baptism is day one of your lifelong journey with Christ.

Scripture says, "Repent and be baptized" (Acts 2:38). It is the first thing we do once we turn from the world and give our life to Jesus.

Baptism demonstrates that, as we go under, our old life is buried with Christ. And as we come up, we are raised to new life in Him.

A new life and faith that cannot be compartmentalized, kept private, or hidden.

WHAT DO I BELIEVE ABOUT JESUS?

This lie—that faith is private—confronts us with the question: What do I believe about Jesus?

Some people treat Jesus as a great moral teacher—someone who said wise things and lived a good life. And if that's all He is, we can easily pick and choose which of His teachings we like, then go on living however we want.

But we know Jesus didn't leave us that option.

He claimed to be the Son of God, the Savior of the world. He claimed authority over life and death, heaven and hell. So, we must decide: Was He telling the truth, or wasn't He?

If He wasn't, then none of this matters. But if He was—if Jesus really is Lord—then everything changes. We cannot simply admire Him. We must surrender to Him. We must reorient our entire life around Him.

This is where casual Christianity, which is all too common today, falls apart. When we confess Jesus as Lord, we're saying, "My faith is not one part of my life—it *is* my life. I belong to Him."

One way people make this public confession is by coming forward to commit their lives to Christ during an altar call. This is a relatively recent phenomenon in church history. It has emerged over the past couple hundred years. One of the reasons it has grown in the West is because it communicates that following Jesus costs something up front.

When you come forward you are publicly committing your life to Christ, risking what others may think of you. It is an opportunity to live your faith out loud, starting in a room full of Christians who are cheering your decision.

Because, if you don't have the courage to acknowledge Jesus as Lord in the church, you certainly won't have the courage to confess Him as Lord in the world.

THE COUNTERFEIT IDENTITY: THE LUKEWARM BELIEVER

The church in Laodicea has the reputation of being the only church about which Jesus had nothing good to say.[3] Located in one of the wealthiest cities and commercial centers at the time, the church was so affluent that it seemed to lack empathy for other first-century churches that struggled to make ends meet or experienced persecution.

One of the major challenges of Laodicea was its lack of a natural water source. To meet the city's needs, aqueducts were built to bring cold water from Colossae, about ten miles away, and hot mineral-rich water from the springs of Hierapolis, six miles to the north.

The water from Hierapolis, while useful for bathing, was not ideal for drinking due to its high mineral content. And by the time either source reached Laodicea, the water had become lukewarm and stale—neither hot enough to soothe nor cold enough to refresh.[4]

In speaking to the church in Laodicea, Jesus drew on this local reality, saying, "I know your deeds, that you are neither cold nor hot. I wish you were either one or the other! So, because you are lukewarm—neither hot nor cold—I am about to spit you out of my mouth (Revelation 3:15–16).

Jesus knows the enemy is on a mission to try and get you to moderate or tame your faith. To become a Lukewarm Believer.

Lukewarm Believers buy into the lie that faith is meant to be kept private, that each of us can keep our faith to ourselves.

It is actually an identity that many believers are attracted to. Not the "lukewarm" title, but the opportunity to have it both ways. To enjoy the benefits of the world and the benefits of the church. A foot in both worlds.

This affects a lot more of us than we think. Especially those of us who arc upwardly mobile and thus more likely to be blind to this dynamic.

Jesus gave the church in Laodicea a strong rebuke: "You say,

'I am rich; I have acquired wealth and do not need a thing.' But you do not realize that you are wretched, pitiful, poor, blind and naked" (verse 17).

When we have so many of our material needs met, we can forget just how dependent we are on God. Our wealth blinds us to our spiritual needs.

And when we surround ourselves with lukewarm believers, we can begin to think this is the norm. We can forget how good cold water tastes.

But God doesn't forget. He wants nothing to do with the lukewarm, complacent faith of cultural Christianity that has one foot in the church and one foot in the world.

NOMINAL CHRISTIANITY

Lukewarm Christianity is really just nominal Christianity.

Nominal Christians are Christians in name only. They accept the label of "Christian" but their life looks no different from the world. There is no evidence of the fruit of the Spirit, no prayer life, no consistent Bible reading or church attendance.

My call to serve in Boston was really a reaction to the nominal Christianity I had witnessed much of my life. At that point, I felt many of the people around me were Christians in name only. They seemed to follow Jesus because it benefited them—they went to church for an hour on Sunday because it increased their social standing or made them feel better about themselves.

Please hear me: Don't believe the lie that your faith can be kept private. You may think this lie hasn't affected you or your church, but consider whether thoughts like these have ever crossed your mind:

- "I would never be someone who would talk about my faith at work."
- "I would never be one of those people who imposes my faith on someone else, especially a friend or neighbor."

The enemy is on a mission to moderate or tame your faith like he did the Laodiceans. They thought they just had a water problem. They didn't realize their real problem was their spiritual condition. Their compartmentalized and privatized faith was nauseating to Jesus. So much so that it caused him to vomit them out.

Keep watch—don't allow the blessings of your life to turn your faith lukewarm.

THE TRUTH: JESUS IS LORD

Let's return to the question, What do I really believe about Jesus?

If He is just another great moral teacher, then we can simply add Him to our existing life.

This is what happens when there is faith without repentance. When there is no public profession of our faith. When we declare Jesus as Savior but not Lord.

To declare "Jesus is Lord" in the first few centuries could easily have cost you your life. The Roman Empire demanded that everyone declare, "Caesar is Lord."

The enemy is on a mission to moderate or tame your faith.

This was not just a political statement but a religious declaration to acknowledge the emperor's divine authority.

To declare anyone else as Lord was viewed as treasonous and a threat to the empire's stability. In fact, above the cross of Christ the soldiers wrote "King of the Jews," which was their way of saying nobody challenges Caesar. This is what made Paul's words to the church in Rome so powerful: "If you declare with your mouth, 'Jesus is Lord,' and believe in your heart that God raised him from the dead, you will be saved" (Romans 10:9).

Declaring it with your mouth publicly, so others could hear, was risky.

Early martyrs like Polycarp, the bishop of Smyrna (AD 155), were killed for refusing to worship the Roman emperor—referred to as Caesar. Polycarp famously said to the Roman proconsul on the eve of his death, "Eighty-six years I have served Him, and He has done me no wrong. How can I blaspheme my King and my Savior?"[5]

When you confess with your mouth "Jesus is Lord," you are saying that He is the name that is above every other name. In my life. In my nation. In our world. He is the only one who has the power to save. And He is now the senior-most authority figure in my life.

If Jesus is not Lord of all, He's not Lord at all.

JESUS IS LORD OF ALL

Paul wrote to the Philippians this first-century hymn:

God exalted him to the highest place
and gave him the name that is above every name,
that at the name of Jesus every knee should bow,

in heaven and on earth and under the earth,
and every tongue acknowledge that Jesus Christ is Lord,
to the glory of God the Father. (Philippians 2:9–11)

Is Jesus Lord over every area of my life?

Or am I a Christian in name only?

Am I compartmentalizing in some way?

Am I drifting in some way?

As I mentioned earlier, one of the enemy's primary strategies is to moderate or tame our faith. To turn Jesus into a helpful assistant rather than Lord. To use faith as a tool to some other end. We begin to believe something not because it's true, but because it benefits us—socially, emotionally, or politically.

For example, we might value Christianity because of its social benefits or moral teachings, but not believe in the actual resurrection of Jesus. We might love the community of the church but quietly reject its core theology. When that happens, Jesus becomes a means to an end—not the end Himself.

The most exciting part of doing life with God is learning to fully yield ourselves to His lordship and authority. To allow Him to lead us rather than vice versa.

I think of someone like Jon in our church, who has learned the joy of a surrendered life. He is a middle-aged entrepreneur who was radically saved and baptized on Easter Sunday. A few months later we had another baptism, and Jon was there, rejoicing with those who were going public with their faith, and remembering God's goodness in his own life. He later sent me the following message describing his reaction:

> I was just so full of joy from the day and went to get some ice cream in Union Market. As I ordered, the peo-

> ple working there said "what is going on with you . . . you are so full of light and energy?" And without thinking I just responded, "I am full of new life . . . I just watched 20 people get baptized today so I am full of new life and the love of the Lord." They just smiled and nodded!

When you have truly confessed Jesus as Lord and surrendered your entire life over to Him, you will no longer treat Jesus as a means to your own end. Money is a good thing, influence is a good thing, sex is a good thing, loving your country is a good thing. But these gifts must be expressed in God-designed ways.

One of the ways to know if you are using God as a means to an end is if your primary concern becomes pursuing one of these other things over and above Christ. God gets reduced to a servant to help you with your latest problem, rather than being worshiped for who He truly is.

This temptation to use God for outcomes—even good ones—isn't just personal. It shows up in our collective expectations too.

We saw this during the Asbury awakening. Some said, "We'll believe it's revival when we see justice." While it's true that real revival leads to social change, there is a danger in demanding visible results before we recognize the transformative power of God's presence. Dwelling in God's presence is not a stage you graduate from once you are eager to improve the world. You never move beyond the basics, you only grow deeper in them. It's a subtle but deadly shift to believe something only if it produces something else, to trust in God's work only when it aligns with your desired outcomes.

THE ROOTS OF REAL REVIVAL

When faith becomes private, it becomes compartmentalized. And once compartmentalized, it's no longer your highest aim. That's when you begin to reduce faith to a means—often to support your latest passion, even if it's a noble one, like making the world a better place.

Screwtape put it plainly: "We do want, and want very much, to make men treat Christianity as a means; preferably, of course, as a means to their own advancement, but, failing that, as a means to anything—even to social justice."[6]

For some Christians, social justice becomes a cover for doing things *for* God instead of walking closely *with* Him. Why does it matter if I'm sleeping with my boyfriend if I'm marching for justice on the weekends? Why do I need to go to church when I'm worshiping God through serving the homeless once a week?

Scripture is clear: God is a God of justice. Inner transformation must lead to outer transformation. And any so-called revival that justifies oppression or sidesteps repentance is not a true encounter with God. The issue isn't Christians committing to biblical justice—that's essential. The danger is when we rush past God's presence in our pursuit of progress. When we substitute impact for intimacy, and we start valuing the *fruits* of our faith more than the *roots*.

The call is not to serve God in the hope that He will fulfill our vision for the world, but to surrender fully to His. True revival doesn't begin by asking God to bless our agenda; it begins by laying our agendas down before Him in worship. God is not looking for performers or professionals. He is looking for worshipers. Men and women who will lay down their agendas and pick up their crosses. This is where revival begins.

When we come before Him with no agenda other than to be in His presence, that's where real heart change happens. And only from that place—of surrendered worship—can God speak to us, refine us, and empower us to manifest His justice and righteousness in the world.

THE BENEFITS OF SURRENDER

The benefits of a truly surrendered life to Jesus are numerous.

It's counterintuitive, but letting go and allowing God to take control is what brings lasting peace. When we stop trying to control everything in our lives, God will steer us in the direction that will most fulfill us and bring Him the most glory.

This is what Paul experienced as he wrote to the Galatians: "I have been crucified with Christ and I no longer live, but Christ lives in me. The life I now live in the body, I live by faith in the Son of God, who loved me and gave himself for me" (Galatians 2:20).

There is real joy in surrender.

One of the most common questions I've been asked as a pastor is, How do I know if something is God's will? With a relationship, with a job, with a possible move. The answer is in fully surrendering to the Lord, which is impossible to do if you are living a compartmentalized life.

In Romans 12, Paul told us that the way to discern God's will is to totally surrender ourselves to God, including our bodies:

> I urge you, brothers and sisters, in view of God's mercy, to offer your bodies as a living sacrifice, holy and pleasing to God—this is your true and proper worship. Do not conform to the pattern of this world, but be trans-

> formed by the renewing of your mind. Then you will be able to test and approve what God's will is—his good, pleasing and perfect will. (verses 1–2)

When we resist the ways of this world, offer ourselves to God as living sacrifices, and release everything we want to have control over, the result is a renewed mind that is able to discern God's perfect and pleasing will for our lives.

When Jesus is truly Lord of my life, it becomes very clear how I should treat my body, how I should relate to money, and how I should steward my influence.

Three of the greatest idols that seek to destroy our worship and get us to compartmentalize our lives are:

Money: Jesus said, "No one can serve two masters. Either you will hate the one and love the other, or you will be devoted to the one and despise the other. You cannot serve both God and money" (Matthew 6:24).

Sex: Paul said, "Do you not know that your bodies are temples of the Holy Spirit, who is in you, whom you have received from God? You are not you own; you were bought at a price. Therefore honor God with your bodies" (1 Corinthians 6:19–20).

Power: Peter said, "Humble yourselves, therefore, under God's mighty hand, that he may lift you up in due time" (1 Peter 5:6).

Imagine your money no longer being a source of anxiety or identity, but a joyful tool in the hands of your Master—freely given, strategically deployed for kingdom impact. Imagine your body as more than something to maintain or indulge, but a sacred dwelling place of the living God, a temple radiating the presence of the Holy Spirit in the everyday. Imagine your ambition and influence no longer driven by the pressure to prove something to the world, but shaped by a posture of humility that trusts God's timing over your own.

What amazing freedom we find in releasing our grip on control! And what peace comes when we trust God with the parts of our lives that once felt too private, too painful, or too difficult to surrender.

The world tells us that fulfillment comes by grasping—grasping for more power, more pleasure, more control. But the gospel tells a different story: Fulfillment comes through surrender. Real life begins when we lay down our agendas and acknowledge Jesus on the throne. That's when our identity stabilizes. Our anxiety diminishes. Our purpose comes into view. And our worship becomes whole.

When Jesus is truly Lord of your life, faith never stays hidden. It overflows into a public witness. The peace and freedom you experience in Christ begin to show up in your relationships, your work, your home, and your everyday conversations.

WHAT PUBLIC FAITH LOOKS LIKE

Not everyone is called to give away everything and go serve on the streets of Boston. But all of us are called to live out our faith in public. A faith that moves beyond Sunday morning and permeates every nook and cranny of our lives.

Too often when people hear the call to "public faith," they imagine something loud or confrontational—like open-air preaching or online theological debates. But public faith isn't about being loud, it's about being real. It's about being honest about who you are, how God is working in your life, and living in such a way that people begin to ask questions.

Let me give you a few examples of what that can look like.

I think of a friend who has a very senior position in the federal government. He was halfway through our ten-week discipleship curriculum called Rooted when I met with him at his workplace, and I asked him how it was going.[7] He said, "Well, everyone here now knows about Rooted." I was puzzled. While he was in a very senior role in charge of tens of thousands of employees, he isn't the sort of personality that I would think would be "loud" about his faith.

So I wondered how everyone knew. He said, "Everyone knows because I have to be in town Wednesday nights. And this has created so many issues with my schedulers that everyone is now wondering what priority in my life is causing me to move heaven and earth to travel back, often internationally, to make my weekly Rooted meeting."

Public faith isn't about being loud, it's about being real.

That piqued curiosity and gave him the opportunity to talk about his church and his faith in an authentic and real way. To share how his faith is the most important thing about his life and how it influences everything, including his schedule. You may not be in a senior position to do something similar, but there are ways you can clearly and winsomely express your faith at work, whether that work is in an office or at home.

I also think of a mom in our church who was already busy raising a toddler and working her corporate job in finance, but was moved by Jesus' command to "love your neighbor." She asked the simple question, "What if Jesus meant I am to love my actual neighbors?" She and her husband had the means to buy a house in their neighborhood of choice, but instead stayed in their rented apartment building because they felt called to love their *actual* neighbors. She is not particularly outgoing, but for over eight years now, they have served that apartment community—hosting events, praying for residents, and sharing the love of Christ in practical ways.

I think about the Uber driver in our church who has spiritual conversations with his passengers on a daily basis. He is always telling me about who he prayed for or invited to church that week. Despite being very open about his faith, he continually gets high ratings from passengers, which is a testimony for how naturally he shares about his love for Christ.

None of these people would call themselves evangelists. They're just ordinary Christians who have decided not to keep their faith to themselves. They've allowed the truth of what Jesus has done to shape how they show up at work, at home, and in everyday conversations. Their witness isn't flashy, but it's faithful. And over time it results in changed lives.

You don't have to be famous to make an impact. You don't need a platform or a theology degree. You just need a story, and the willingness to share it.

THE COMMITMENT: SHARING YOUR STORY (BOLD STORYTELLING)

The good news? You already have a story worth sharing.

Sharing your story is simply talking to others about what God is doing in your life. You don't have to force it or script it. You've already got the material—your doubts and breakthroughs, your struggles, the prayers God has answered and the ones you're still waiting on. These moments are sacred but not secret. They're meant to be shared.

This is how we resist the temptation to privatize our faith

or become lukewarm. We consistently practice what believers have done for two thousand years, which is to share our faith by actively sharing our story.

The problem is, most of us don't have the confidence to share our faith. This is why we need help. And the good news is that Jesus promises it! Jesus said: "You will receive power when the Holy Spirit comes on you; and you will be my witnesses in Jerusalem, and in all Judea and Samaria, and to the ends of the earth" (Acts 1:8).

He said, "You will be my witnesses." In other words, "You *will* share your story."

And you will not be able to confine it to a single geographic area or even one area of your life. You will not be able to confine it to just one story.

God never intended for there to be two tiers of Christians: some who share their faith and some who do not. While some are particularly gifted at evangelism, all of us are called to share our faith.

The amazing thing about the Christian faith is that we all get to participate. We all get to receive God's undeserved grace. We all get to practice spiritual disciplines. We all get to receive spiritual gifts. We all get to serve and play a role in advancing God's kingdom.

When you share your story, you are sharing what God has done and is doing in your life. This includes how you came to saving faith and the ways you have seen and heard God at work in your life.

Just like there is nobody on this earth that looks just like you, there is nobody that has a story just like yours. God has given you a unique story and you have a responsibility to share it with others!

Christian storytelling is different from secular storytelling.

For one, you are part of a *bigger story*. Start by remembering what God has done. You are just one small piece, and so, as you tell your story you are sharing how your story fits in with God's. In fact, this is what Peter did in Acts 2 when he testified, "Fellow Israelites, listen to this: Jesus of Nazareth was a man accredited by God to you by miracles, wonders and signs, which God did among you through him, as you yourselves know" (verse 22).

He went on to say that Jesus was crucified, but "God has raised this Jesus to life, and we are all witnesses of it" (verse 32).

When you share your story, you are not just remembering what God has done in your lifetime, but what God has done in history.

Second, Christian storytelling requires *vulnerability*. Your story is attractive because it is marked by struggle, past and present. Paul said he was chief among sinners. He didn't hide that he used to persecute Christians. Peter didn't hide the fact that he had denied Jesus at His most important hour. Scripture says, "[God's] power is made perfect in weakness" (2 Corinthians 12:9).

Don't just share your highlight reel. Share difficult and messy realities. Share honestly about your failures and the many times Jesus picked you back up.

Every summer, our church creates space for people to share in a series we call *This Is My Story*. They speak vulnerably about the hardest parts of their journey, their biggest questions, their deepest obstacles. It's become one of our most impactful series, because again and again, we're reminded that God meets us in our lowest places.

Vulnerability opens the door for the Holy Spirit to move. It makes space for people to believe—maybe for the first time—that there's a God who sees their struggles.

Third, Christian storytellers are different from secular storytellers in how we *listen*. Of course, you are listening to God's story, but you are also listening to other people's stories. Listen with curiosity. With patience. Your genuine interest in their stories gives you the credibility to share with others what God has done in your life. Even if they do not share your faith.

Recently a young mom in our church was diagnosed with cancer. Instead of keeping her diagnosis private, she opened up and shared with her co-workers. She didn't start with a theological argument or a dramatic altar call. She started by simply sharing what God was teaching her in this difficult season, how He was helping her navigate anxiety, parent her son, and how her faith was giving her peace. That vulnerable, ordinary moment sparked several conversations that eventually led to two of her co-workers coming to church—and back to faith.

Her story wasn't polished. It wasn't perfect. But it was honest. And the Holy Spirit used it.

You don't need a microphone or a podcast to share your story. It can happen over lunch with a friend who's walking through a hard time. It can show up in a small-group moment when someone finally opens up about their doubt, and you offer a word of hope from your own journey. Sometimes it's an Instagram post where you reflect on something God has done in your life, or a simple offer to pray with a co-worker who's struggling. You might even find it bubbling up in a casual moment—like during lunch break at work, around the dinner table at a family gathering, or with your barista who keeps asking why you're always so joyful on Sunday afternoons.

You don't have to tell your whole story at once. Sometimes it starts with a sentence. Sometimes a question. What matters is your willingness to speak.

The more you share, the more natural it becomes. And the more you will build your own faith. Paul told Philemon, "I pray that you may be active in sharing your faith, so that you will have a full understanding of every good thing we have in Christ" (Philemon v. 6, NIV, 1984).

As you share, you'll realize that your story—your honest, imperfect, unfolding story—might be exactly what someone else needs to hear to believe that God sees them too.

WE NEED POWER

A public faith begins with a willingness to share our story. But it is not enough to simply *desire* to share our story; we need power from on high.

There is just too much we are up against. For one, most of us have a real fear of honestly sharing about what we have gone through. Especially publicly.

We also fear sharing anything about faith or religion that could come across as "exclusive" to our co-workers or friends. There is real fear of being canceled.

But even more than that, we're up against the devil himself. The enemy does not want us to share our stories. Why? Because as the book of Revelation puts it, we overcome the enemy "by the blood of the Lamb [Jesus] and by the word of [our] testimony" (12:11). That's how we win. Jesus has already done His part. Now it's time for us to do ours. To share our story.

Jesus said, "You will receive power when the Holy Spirit comes on you." Then, in that same moment, He said, "You will be my witnesses" (Acts 1:8).

"Witness" in the basic Greek, *mártus,* means "one who shares what they have seen and heard." The word *martyr* comes from the same root, meaning someone who bears witness to their faith, that results in death.[8]

Jesus understands that when it comes to our being a witness, we need more than a pep talk or a parable.

We need power.

Power to enable us to translate desires into action. Power to boldly share our love for God by talking about what we've seen and heard Him do in our life.

Peter and John were filled with the Holy Spirit and couldn't stop sharing their story even when they were arrested and brought before the very powerful Sanhedrin. They said, "We cannot help speaking about what we have seen and heard" (Acts 4:20).

If you really love something, you will talk about it.

Even when it's risky.

My prayer is that you would have the power to resist living a private, compartmentalized life and actively share your story, wherever you have opportunity.

The world is waiting for believers who truly live out what we say we believe. Where our faith cannot be hidden, compartmentalized, or considered lukewarm.

DISCUSSION AND REFLECTION QUESTIONS

Lie 3: Faith Is Private

1. **Compartmentalized Faith**

   In what areas have you compartmentalized your faith from the rest of your life? How has this affected your relationship with God and others? What challenges do you face in integrating faith into all areas of your life?
2. **Comfort vs. Dependence**

   How does pursuing a comfortable life make it harder to fully rely on God? How have you experienced spiritual growth through either discomfort or dependence on Him?
3. **Faith in Action**

   In what ways do you publicly live out your faith? How might fear or social pressure prevent you from being open about your relationship with Jesus?
4. **Lukewarm Christianity**

   Jesus condemns lukewarm faith in Revelation 3:15–16. How do you recognize lukewarm tendencies in your own life, and what steps can you take to rekindle a vibrant faith?
5. **Sharing Your Story**

   How comfortable are you with sharing your story of faith with others? What holds you back, and how might the Holy Spirit empower you to overcome these obstacles?
6. **Jesus as Lord**

   What does it mean to you to declare "Jesus is Lord" in every area of your life? Are there any areas you find particularly hard to surrender to His authority?
7. **Faith in Community**

   How does being part of a Christian community help keep your faith from becoming private or lukewarm?

8. **Countering Nominal Christianity**

   What's the difference between being a nominal Christian and fully embracing Jesus as Lord? How can you help others move beyond cultural Christianity?

9. **Power of Testimony**

   Revelation 12:11 says, "They triumphed . . . by the word of their testimony." How has sharing your testimony affected others, or how has hearing someone else's story affected you?

10. **Breaking the Lie**

    The lie says, "Faith is private." How can you intentionally live out your faith in public spaces (work, school, community) without being preachy or pushy?

4

WHEN THE BIBLE GETS EDITED

From Selective Reading to Wholehearted Engagement

> He [your patient] doesn't think of doctrines as primarily "true" or "false," but as "academic" or "practical," "outworn" or "contemporary," "conventional" or "ruthless." Jargon, not argument, is your best ally in keeping him from the Church.
>
> —*The Screwtape Letters,* Letter 1

In the early seventies a group of seminary students led by Jim Wallis grew frustrated by the lack of engagement in churches around issues of poverty and justice. To raise awareness, they decided to read through the entire Bible and highlight every reference they found to wealth, poverty, and justice. By the time they made it through, they had highlighted more than two thousand verses.

Then they took scissors and cut out all those references to the poor. As you can imagine, the Bible was in shreds. Wallis then went around preaching in churches across the country, holding up the tattered Bible and saying, "Brothers and sisters, this is the American Bible. It's full of holes."[1]

It was a prophetic word to the church of how picking and choosing which parts of the Bible to believe compromises our faith.

What began as selective silence on justice has now shifted toward selective silence on sexuality. Both distortions emerge from the same root: discomfort with parts of God's Word.

> This lie is about valuing experience over truth.

Every generation faces the temptation to eliminate or ignore passages that feel inconvenient or offensive in their cultural moment. Some want to cut out what Scripture says about justice and compassion for the vulnerable. Others want to remove what it says about God's design for holiness, identity, and relationships. And all this selectivity is usually done in the name of love.

These actions are the fruit of believing a deeper lie.

The lie that the Bible is outdated.

THE LIE: THE BIBLE IS OUTDATED

I used to field questions on a weekly basis with newcomers who would ask us our church's position on marriage. For many years I tried to win the person over by engaging them on the level of their question.

In fact, I wrote a sixty-page paper about our traditional view of sexuality and marriage to better respond winsomely to people in our church who were struggling to hold on to the orthodox Christian view in our changing times. I would then host a packed-out three-week class where I would teach and engage with folks on this topic. Then members of the church would write their position on marriage, having to make a biblical case either for or against same-sex romantic relationships.

After reading hundreds of these papers, and engaging in thousands of conversations, what I have realized is that this conversation is rarely about sexuality at its core. It is about something further upstream. It is about whether God's Word can be trusted as the final authority in our lives.

When the secular worldview begins to take root, we begin to question any and all authority, including the Bible.

The secular worldview rejects any form of external authority in favor of personal freedom and autonomy. For example, in many classrooms today, children are encouraged to find their own truth or speak their truth, regardless of whether it aligns with reality or moral absolutes. Even in parenting, the highest value is often placed on affirming a child's feelings rather than forming their character. This shift reflects the deeper worldview that no authority—whether parental, educational, or divine—should interfere with personal autonomy.

This rejection of external authority in exchange for personal autonomy is the original lie from Genesis 3. Since the secular worldview believes humans are inherently good and not fallen, the goal is to maximize personal liberty. To throw off any worldview or institution that could limit our ability to find our own truth.

This is what makes the authority of Scripture so troubling to secular Christians. And so, Scripture takes a back seat and must be reinterpreted or even discarded when it is not compatible.

Few issues divide Christians and churches more deeply today than how we view the authority of Scripture. Some of the most influential figures contributing to this shift are authors and teachers, like Pete Enns, who invite readers to rethink biblical inspiration through the lens of modern scholarship. Nadia Bolz-Weber recasts Christian sexual ethics entirely around personal autonomy. Jen Hatmaker has publicly shifted toward affirming theology, influencing many evangelicals to reinterpret Scripture through emotional and relational lenses. Each presents a form of faith that resonates with cultural values—but often at the cost of biblical authority.

The way this issue of biblical authority is discussed, however, is quite subtle. Most progressive-leaning Christians would never acknowledge that they lack confidence in the authority of the Bible. They would never cede that ground and lose the only audience they really have, which is other Christians.

Instead of coming out and saying, "I no longer believe the Bible has authority," they usually start more subtly. A friend once told me about a conversation he had with his sister, who grew up in the same church he did. When a close friend of hers came out as gay, her entire relationship with Scripture began to shift. She started highlighting verses about love and inclusion, saying things like, "Jesus never mentioned homosexuality," and "That part of Paul sounds more like his culture than like Jesus."

She wasn't trying to pick a fight or abandon her faith. She was trying to protect someone she cared about—and that desire began reshaping how she read the Bible. Before long, the conversation wasn't about biblical authority at all. It was about feelings, fairness, and the fear of seeming unloving. The text hadn't changed—but the lens had.

Over the many years of engaging in this debate even on the national level, among the most articulate and respected leaders on the affirming side, I've never heard anyone make anything close to a compelling *biblical* case for same-sex marriage.

The shift from the Old to the New Testament is not toward leniency but toward a more profound purity. Jesus didn't lower the standard—He brought it closer, straight to the heart. Jesus raised the bar, saying that if you look at a woman lustfully you've already committed adultery with her in your heart.[2]

Paul agreed. Romans 1 talks about how people ended up exchanging God's truth for a lie by exchanging natural sexual relations with the opposite sex for unnatural relations with the same sex.[3] Paul warned in 1 Corinthians 6 to flee from sexual immorality because our bodies are temples of the Holy Spirit. He wrote that "wrongdoers will not inherit the kingdom of God" and specifically includes among them the sexually immoral, idolaters, adulterers, men who have sex with men, thieves, the greedy, drunkards, slanderers, and swindlers.[4]

The conversation today is seldom about the clear teaching of the Bible, but rather about feelings, desires, and experiences.

The question raised today is something like: Why does the Bible seem to oppose LGBTQ+ relationships when "love is love"? Do the authors of the Bible really understand the range of our human experiences today? Do they really understand the concept of committed, monogamous same-sex relationships? Of a society that legally allows same-sex marriage?

A conversation around sexuality will quickly reveal whether the secular worldview of expressive individualism now holds more authority for the person you are talking to than the Bible.

There was a guy in our church who had always held a high view of Scripture. He led a men's group, served regularly, and genuinely sought to live with integrity. But then one of his closest friends came out to him. They had been through everything together—college, job changes, even spiritual milestones. The moment felt like a fork in the road. He told me later, "I just couldn't imagine telling him that his love for another man was wrong. It felt like I had to choose between loyalty to him and loyalty to what I'd always believed."

This is more common than we realize. People aren't always rejecting Scripture outright—they're reframing it, consciously or unconsciously, through the lens of emotional resonance and relational loyalty. That's why this moment requires spiritual clarity and pastoral compassion. Not to shame, but to shepherd. To walk people back to a confidence in the authority of God's Word—even when it costs something.

If issues of sexuality were the only ones being raised then we could just zero in on that specific topic, but they are not. There are many more questions being raised today that can challenge one's belief in the authority of Scripture. These questions used to be largely concentrated in progressive urban areas, but more recently they have spread to every geographic area, thanks to the internet.

Here are some of the most common ones:

- If God is good, why is the world so broken? (problem of suffering)
- How can I believe in the Bible's creation story when science says otherwise? (a perceived threat to human progress)
- How can Christianity be true if other religions also claim to lead to God? (a perceived threat to inclusivity)
- How can I trust a book that has been used to justify slavery and oppression? (a perceived threat to justice)
- What about the problem of hell? (problem of judgment and eternity)

These are genuine questions people have been asking for centuries. Questions related to science, salvation, and injustice. The difference is that now these questions are increasingly being asked by Christians—many of whom have not been well equipped to wrestle with them or to truly know what Scripture teaches. In the absence of that grounding, a cultural narrative often fills the vacuum—one that frames the Bible not as the solution but as the problem.

At the root of so many of these questions is a belief that the people who wrote the Bible did not understand what we are facing in our world today. They didn't understand the range of our human experience today. They didn't understand the extent of injustice today.

Therefore, the Bible is outdated.

THE COUNTER IDENTITY: THE SELECTIVE CHRISTIAN

When we believe the lie that the Bible is outdated, we start picking and choosing which parts to believe.

We don't call it that, of course. We say things like, "I'm not leaving the faith—I still love Jesus. I just don't agree with everything the Bible says." It feels more like curating than compromising. Like following or unfollowing people on social media, we assemble a custom spiritual feed based on our preferences.

That's how many sincere believers slowly become what I call "Selective Christians"—not just wrestling with honest doubts, but forming a pattern of filtering God's Word through cultural lenses and personal preferences.

This often starts subtly with good intentions.

For example, there was a woman in our church who had grown up in a conservative evangelical setting. She had memorized Scripture as a child and had always considered herself grounded in the Word. But when her brother came out as gay, everything changed. She began to ask questions—about love, inclusion, and what kind of God she believed in. "I know what the Bible says," she told me one day, "but it just doesn't feel right anymore. My brother is the most loving, kind, and faithful person I know. I can't accept a version of Christianity that won't affirm his identity."

That was a turning point.

When we believe the lie that the Bible is outdated, we start picking and choosing which parts to believe.

She didn't renounce her faith. She still went to church. She still quoted Scripture. But little by little, she began to interpret the Bible through her emotional allegiance to her brother. She started avoiding certain texts and only affirming the ones that resonated with her. In time, she stopped referring to Jesus as Lord, and instead described Him as a model of "radical inclusion."

This is where many Christians find themselves today: struggling to reconcile their faith with their emotional ties. Rather than reject Christianity, they quietly reshape it. But what begins as empathy can turn into erosion. Instead of conforming our lives to Scripture, we conform Scripture to our lives.

And when that happens long enough, we don't just develop new views—we adopt a new identity.

This identity, the Selective Christian, is shaped more by culture than by Christ. It straddles two worlds—wanting to belong to the church but not submit to all its teachings. It affirms Jesus in name but edits His Word in practice. It's often well-meaning, even tender-hearted, but it's ultimately a counterfeit.

Now, let me be clear: Asking hard questions doesn't make you a Selective Christian. Having doubts doesn't disqualify you from being a disciple. We all wrestle. We all wonder. And many of us need to deconstruct the poor theology we were handed in order to reconstruct a biblical faith. That's part of the journey.

But the danger comes when wrestling turns into rewriting—when we no longer submit to the Bible, but critique it from a distance.

In this mindset, Scripture becomes something to analyze and challenge, rather than God's Word to obey. Verses are not seen as true or false, but rather as helpful or harmful, inspiring or outdated. Just as Screwtape advises, the goal is to get Christians to view doctrine not as "truth," but as "academic" "outworn" or "ruthless." That's how the enemy keeps people in church buildings while leading them away from biblical truth.[5]

Again, this shift is often gradual. One minute, you're highlighting verses in your Bible. The next, you're silently ignoring ones that don't fit your worldview.

You still quote the Psalms, but you've quietly set aside the virgin birth. You love the idea of resurrection hope, but not the bodily resurrection. You show up for Easter, sing about light and life, but inwardly doubt the return of Christ.

The data reflects this drift.

A Barna study found that just 17 percent of "practicing Christians who consider their faith important and attend church regularly actually have a biblical worldview."[6]

They found among these practicing Christians:

- 61% agree with beliefs rooted in New Spirituality.
- 54% resonate with postmodernist views.
- 29% believe ideas rooted in secularism.

And almost half of practicing Christian millennials (47 percent) "agree at least somewhat that it is *wrong* to share one's personal beliefs with someone of a different faith in hopes that they will one day share the same faith."[7]

That's not just a shift in opinion—that's a shift in authority.

Once the Bible is no longer the authority, cultural values take its place. And soon the church is filled with people who profess faith but deny its core truths.

It's a form of Christianity with no power to save or transform.

What happens when a church is shaped by this? The doctrine becomes diluted. The calls to repentance go silent. The sermons avoid sacrifice or submission. Worship becomes a mood. Justice is defined more by the latest headline than by Micah 6:8.

And the next generation watches—and walks away.

Because when church becomes indistinguishable from culture, there's nothing left to call people to. No repentance. No transformation. Just good vibes and spiritual slogans.

This kind of selective faith is not confined to the left or right. Both progressive and conservative circles are vulnerable. One camp may elevate inclusion above truth; the other may ignore justice and mercy while championing morality. But both end up reshaping the gospel in their image.

At the root is the same spirit: the spirit of this age that elevates personal autonomy above divine authority.

And that's how the Bible gets edited. Not with scissors, but with silence. We emphasize the passages that affirm our values. We avoid the ones that challenge our habits. And slowly, without realizing it, we begin to follow a version of Jesus who always agrees with us—rather than the Jesus who calls us to take up our cross.

But when we strip out the parts of Scripture we don't like—

whether about sin, judgment, sexuality, or sacrifice—we strip the gospel and the cross of its power.[8]

That's why progressive Christianity never reproduces. It may linger for a generation, helped by an endowment or nostalgic tradition, but it won't last. There is nothing compelling about a church that affirms everything and calls for nothing.

Selective Christianity is often the on-ramp to progressive Christianity—which in time becomes the on-ramp to post-Christianity.

The stakes couldn't be higher.

At the very root of the problem is the spirit of this age, which teaches us to value personal autonomy and the authority of self. And that spirit is more destructive and even more powerful than the furthest right-wing or left-wing politics.

For example, those who are not submitted to the authority of Scripture tend to take their favorite virtue, such as inclusion, and make it the most dominant theme in Scripture. They selectively read Scripture to eliminate parts that are not consistent with this favorite theme. In this scenario, doctrines like human depravity, atonement, resurrection, and the second coming of Christ are severely compromised, ignored, or completely eliminated.

By contrast, I grew up in an era where issues of poverty and justice were being eliminated from Bibles by Selective Christians. I never heard a sermon talking about God's heart for the orphan, the widow, the stranger. I never heard about how connected our spiritual growth is to being able to recognize Jesus in the face of the poor.[9]

In either case, we've remade the gospel in our own image such that it is no longer good news.

THE AUTHORITY OF SELF OR SCRIPTURE?

Every Christian today must ask themselves, "What do I really believe about the Bible?"

Beneath this question are some other important questions: "Do I believe in revealed truth?" "Do I believe in any authority higher than my own personal experience and opinions?" These topics are related. Because if I don't believe in revealed truth then I can't believe in the authority of God's Word.

There is a battle happening today between the authority of self and the authority of Scripture. Western society, over the last five hundred years, has increasingly valued self-expression and individual autonomy. So much so that we see these as ultimate goals. When self-expression and individual autonomy are elevated as our highest goal, traditional notions of truth will be eroded and eventually discarded. And this has a distinct impact on how we see ourselves.

By and large, people in the West no longer root their identity in their faith. Instead, cultural forces train us to center our feelings and desires. We tend to see humans and their desires as intrinsically good, rather than fallen and in need of redemption.

Secular culture elevates personal experience over objective truth. As a result, we often reject anything imposed on us from the outside that challenges or restricts our sense of personal autonomy. In this line of thinking, if God is allowed to exist at all, He must exist for us, rather than vice versa.

In this cultural environment, historic truth then gets reshaped to avoid anything that jeopardizes our preferred feelings and desires. Traditions and truth are dismissed and labeled as either oppressive or outdated.

Today, most people view purpose and truth as things we

get to define for ourselves. In this view, there is no transcendent authority to which I am accountable who will judge me based on my actions or beliefs.

Anything in society or especially in the faith community that suppresses the heartfelt desires of my "authentic self" must be rejected. The highest truth is to be my authentic self and to follow my inner desires.

It is within this culture of radical expressive individualism that someone can say, "I feel like I am a woman trapped in a man's body" and have this statement not only respected but celebrated.[10]

We are swimming in a secular culture that affects our view of authority and tradition more than we like to admit.

It is within this secular culture where the clear and unified teaching of the church for the last two thousand years around sexuality and marriage can be suddenly changed by a denominational decree.[11] For example, the United Church of Christ, the Episcopal Church, the Presbyterian Church (USA), the Evangelical Lutheran Church in America, and the United Methodist Church have all changed their positions on gay marriage in the last twenty years.[12]

THE TRUTH: THE BIBLE IS GOD'S WORD

To believe in the authority of Scripture is to believe that the Bible is the Word of God. To believe it is entirely accurate, complete, and reliable—without errors.

It means we believe the Bible is God's Word to all people for all times.

It means we give the Bible more authority in our life than our experiences, our own understanding, and our own tradition. Praise God for our experiences, for our minds, and for our godly traditions. God uses each of those things to reveal truth to us. But ultimately when we are trying to discern if something is true or false, we look to God's Word. We submit ourselves to its authority.[13]

Yet the issue is deeper than whether we just believe in the authority of Scripture.

The deeper issue is whether we believe in the *authority of God*—in God's authority to reveal truth, define reality, and have the final say. Whether we believe that He is the Alpha and Omega, the beginning and end, the One who is all-powerful and all-knowing. Whether we believe that from Him, and to Him, and through Him are all things. And whether we believe that He is the one who spoke and gave us His Word.

The question we must grapple with is whether we believe God has done more than just give us His Word.

The Word of God points to the Word made flesh: God's Son, Jesus Christ.[14]

Paul wrote in Colossians 1:17–19:

> He [Jesus] is before all things, and in him all things hold together. And he is the head of the body, the church; he is the beginning and the firstborn from among the dead, so that in everything he might have the *supremacy.* For God was pleased to have all his fullness dwell in him.

The authority of God. The authority of Jesus. The authority of Scripture. They are all connected. This is very good news in a world where everything seems subjective, where truth is personal, and everyone is choosing their own adventure. In this cultural moment, we must wrestle with Jesus' words:

John 8:31–32: "If you hold to my teaching, you are really my disciples. Then you will know the truth, and the *truth* will set you free."
John 14:6: "I am the way and the *truth* and the life."

Jesus didn't give us the option to pick and choose which parts of the Bible we like. Matthew's gospel ends with some of the resurrected Christ's last words before ascending to heaven:

> Therefore go and make disciples of all nations, baptizing them in the name of the Father and of the Son and of the Holy Spirit, and teaching them to obey *everything* I have commanded you. (Matthew 28:19–20)

Jesus didn't make His commands optional or open to personal preference. He is the one who created us and knows what is best for us.

Consider Paul's words to Timothy:

> *All Scripture* is God-breathed and is useful for teaching, rebuking, correcting and training in righteousness, so that the servant of God may be thoroughly equipped for every good work. (2 Timothy 3:16–17)

This is an area where you have to discern the specific ways you are likely to be tempted. There is a spiritual battle going on that is working to weaken your faith by watering down the influence and authority of God and His Word in your life.

You must be strong, stand firm, and put on the full armor of God, including, "the *belt of truth* buckled around your waist" (Ephesians 6:14).

Jesus didn't give us the option to pick and choose which parts of the Bible we like.

The enemy will attack you at your very center, which is why you need God's truth around your core.

Paul talked about how leaders are given to help us mature spiritually in the body of Christ so that we are not tossed back and forth by every new teaching, but instead are able to speak the truth in love.[15]

The early church understood the importance of adhering to the apostles' teaching. In fact, the first evidence of the Spirit's presence in the church after Pentecost is that they devoted themselves to the apostles' teaching.[16]

These teachings would soon become the pages of our New Testament.

The psalmist highlighted the centrality of God's Word throughout Psalm 119, offering prayers such as, "I have hidden your word in my heart that I might not sin against you" (verse 11) and "Your word is a lamp for my feet, a light on my path" (verse 105).

God spoke through the prophet Isaiah, promising that when He sends His Word, it will not return to Him void, but will accomplish the purposes for which He sent it.[17]

THE COMMITMENT: SUBMITTING TO GOD'S WORD (BIBLE ENGAGEMENT)

If the root of the problem is drifting from the authority of God's Word, then the solution must be more than doctrinal agreement—it must be daily immersion. We don't overcome selective Christianity by simply winning arguments, but by forming habits. The most faithful response to the lie that the Bible is outdated is not just to defend its truth but to live by it. That begins with Bible engagement: a consistent, Spirit-led encounter with God's Word that trains us to love, think, and act like Jesus.

It's not enough to own a Bible, or even believe that it is the Word of God. We must engage with it regularly. The way to counter the pull of selective Christianity is through a daily commitment to Scripture. To dive into all of God's Word and allow it to speak to you. To approach the Bible not as a critic but as a disciple—someone who holds together the biblical themes of both truth and love.

The Bible is the bestselling book of all time.[18] There is a Bible in almost every household. Yet research shows that among Americans:

- 50% never or rarely engage Scripture
- 16% engage a few times a year to once a month max
- 18% engage 1–3 times a week
- 16% engage four or more times a week[19]

Several years ago there was a study conducted by the Center for Bible Engagement called "The Power of Four Effect."[20] They found that the life of someone who engages Scripture four or more times a week looks radically different from the life of someone who does not.

"Engage" means to read, study, memorize, or be exposed to Scripture personally, in church services, or in small groups.

Someone who engages the Bible four or more times a week is:

- 228% more likely to share their faith with others
- 59% less likely to view pornography
- 59% less likely to have sex outside of marriage
- 30% less likely to struggle with loneliness

They found that the consequences of biblical illiteracy are:

- Spiritually immaturity
- Susceptiblity to false teaching and conspiracy theories
- Increased likelihood of participating in unbiblical behaviors, such as gambling, getting drunk, and oppressing the poor

The key is four times or more a week. Four is the tipping point.

In fact, the study found that the lives of those who engaged the Bible one to three days of the week are statistically the same as the lives of non-believers. Meaning you can be exposed to Scripture in church on Sundays and in your Bible study each week, but that is not enough. You need to be spending time in Scripture on your own if you expect your life to look different from the world.

It has to be the majority of your week. And if you are an extrovert like me, the good news is that all of your Bible encounters don't have to be alone.

A practice that has increased my Bible engagement is reading through the entire Bible each year. Every morning, I start by reading the Old Testament and New Testament passages for the day. This helps ensure I am reading all of God's Word each year and not just the parts I am most drawn to. It helps me learn to wrestle with the difficult passages each year and to first do so from a devotional level before academically or intellectually.

I also enjoy doing the Bible in a Year plan in community with others. Each year I have about a hundred people go through the Bible with me and share their reflections each day on the YouVersion Bible App of which verses spoke to them. There is power in knowing that you are reading the same thing each day with people who share your values. It helps encourage me and hold me accountable.

Our access to the Bible has never been easier. For most of us, we can access the Bible anywhere, on any device, at any time.

There is more access to the Bible than ever before, but one of our challenges, if you are like me, is learning to prioritize God's Word over the many other words I am processing each day. It's too easy for God's words to get lost in the mix.

A disciple comes to Scripture with humility and hunger.
A Selective Christian comes to it with scissors.

Research now shows that the average American today processes as much information in one day as someone from the 1920s might have processed in an entire year. With the internet, social media, and twenty-four-hour news cycles, we are exposed to an immense flow of data. We have constant access to information. The average person processes around seventy-four gigabytes of information daily, which is the equivalent of watching nine full-length movies a day.[21] Most of the world now uses social media, spending an average of two hours and twenty minutes on it each day.[22]

In his book *The Shallows,* Nicholas Carr shares how the internet is reshaping the way we think, read, and process information.

The internet is literally rewiring our brain. The constant switching between tasks and skimming of information is producing shallow thinking and making it much harder for us to engage in deep, focused thought.[23] Can you relate?

That's why you can wish a friend or co-worker a happy birthday online in the morning, and then see them later and forget it is their birthday.

We have lost our ability to focus and read deeply. And this is affecting our ability to engage deeply when it comes to the Bible. The issue today is not so much access, it's engagement. This is why the Bible can still be the bestselling book of all time but be read by only a small percentage of the population.

Here are a few tips for how you can increase your Bible engagement:

- **Set a time.** Many Christians who read the Bible regularly make it their priority first thing in the morning.[24] I was taught "Bible before belly."
- **Read a Psalm daily.** These are prayers you can easily pray yourself.
- **Read a Gospel chapter daily.** Soak in the teachings of Jesus.
- **Read in community.** Start a Bible in a Year plan and invite others to join you.
- **Download the Bible on all your devices.** This helps your engagement levels when you travel or have a long day, to experience on your commute.
- **Use the Audio feature.** Listen to the Bible on a walk, workout, or drive.

Engaging deeply with all of God's Word is not optional. It is essential.

When we neglect the Scriptures—or only engage with them sporadically—we become vulnerable to false teaching, shallow faith, and spiritual drift. And when we approach the Bible just to affirm what we already think, rather than to be shaped by it, we are no longer following Jesus. We are following ourselves.

The Bible is not a buffet of inspirational quotes or moral suggestions to pick and choose as we like. It is the revealed Word of God—sharper than any double-edged sword. It cuts to the heart of who we are, exposing our motives, correcting our course, and guiding us into truth (Hebrews 4:12).

That's why Jesus didn't say, "Hold to the parts that make sense to you." He said, "If you hold to my teaching, you are really my disciples. Then you will know the truth, and the truth will set you free" (John 8:31–32).

This is what separates a disciple from a Selective Christian. A disciple comes to Scripture with humility and hunger. A Selective Christian comes to it with scissors. A disciple allows the Word of God to shape their heart and behavior. A Selective Christian reshapes the Word to fit their preferences.

This lie—that the Bible is outdated—is nothing new. It's the same ancient deception whispered in the garden: "Did God really say?" It appeals to our desire for autonomy and control. But it always leads to spiritual ruin.

Because when we lose confidence in the Bible, we eventually lose the power of the gospel. We may still gather, still sing, or still pray—but without God's Word as our authority, we will have a form of godliness while denying its power (2 Timothy 3:5).

Jesus didn't give us the option to pick and choose which parts of His teaching we obey.

Jesus is the one who made us. He knows what is best for us. And His Word is true—for all people, in all cultures, at all times.

We don't need a new word. We need a renewed reverence for the Word we've already been given.

Because when we lose confidence in God's Word, we don't just lose our way—we lose our witness. And the ones who suffer most are often the poor—which is the focus of the next chapter.

DISCUSSION AND REFLECTION QUESTIONS

Lie 4: The Bible Is Outdated

1. **Relevance of Scripture**
   How would you respond to the claim that the Bible is outdated and doesn't address the complexities of modern life?
2. **Selective Belief**
   Have you ever been tempted to pick and choose which parts of the Bible to believe? What factors influence this tendency?
3. **Authority of Experience vs. Scripture**
   How do you balance the authority of personal experiences with the authority of Scripture? When have you felt these two in conflict?
4. **The Power of Truth**
   What does it mean to submit to the Bible as the "final authority"? How does this challenge cultural values like autonomy and self-expression?
5. **Critic or Disciple**
   Screwtape warns about treating Scripture as "academic" rather than "true." How can you approach the Bible with humility rather than criticism?
6. **Hot Topics in Faith**
   Why do discussions about topics like sexuality or justice often reveal deeper questions about biblical authority? How should Christians approach these issues?
7. **Cultural Pressures**
   How do societal values like inclusivity or "love is love" influence the way people interpret the Bible? What are the dangers of adapting Scripture to fit cultural norms?

8. **The Practice of Bible Reading**

   What has been your experience with reading the Bible consistently? What practices or tools have helped you engage deeply with Scripture?

9. **Engaging the Whole Bible**

   Have you ever read through the entire Bible? If not, what has held you back? What strategies have helped you engage with challenging passages?

10. **Communicating Truth in Love**

    How can you effectively share the truth of Scripture with someone who feels it is outdated or irrelevant without alienating them?

5

WHEN JUSTICE GETS HIJACKED

From Armchair Activism to Biblical Justice

> Let him do anything but act. No amount of piety in his imagination and affections will harm us if we can keep it out of his will . . . The more often he feels without acting, the less he will be able ever to act, and, in the long run, the less he will be able to feel.
>
> —*The Screwtape Letters,* Letter 13

In ancient Rome, families across the empire often abandoned unwanted newborns—especially girls or children with disabilities—on the outskirts of cities in a brutal practice called "exposing." Parents carried these infants beyond the city walls and left them to die from the elements or wild animals.

Christians, who were a persecuted minority at the time, made a practice of going outside the city walls, finding these children, and bringing them home, sometimes even raising them as their own. This practice has remained throughout church history as Christians have taken in neglected or abused children.[1]

When we were in the early days of planting The District Church, the city came to us asking for help mobilizing churches to respond to the foster care crisis. There simply were not enough foster and adoptive homes to respond to the need.

For about a year we engaged in conversations with the city but thought our engagement could remain at the "canned food drive" or "coat drive" level. We were in no position to help with a city-wide response given that we were in the most demanding years of a church start-up. Furthermore, I didn't feel qualified to help lead the effort. Yes, I was an adoptive and foster parent myself, but I was new to this city—and as a white man, I didn't reflect the cultural background of many of the families these foster children came from.

This lie is about secular justice.

But as I was about to find out, we can't run from God. In fact, God woke me up one night and wouldn't let me go back to sleep. I got up and wrote down the vision.

It was so clear. The dream was for more families to be waiting for children than children waiting for families. The dream was to reverse the foster care wait list. James 1:27 was our call—to care for orphans in their distress.

We named the initiative DC127.[2] Since 2010, we have worked with more than fifty churches to reduce the foster care list in D.C. from over two thousand children to less than five hundred children today!

When the head of D.C. Child and Family Services Agency first approached us about leading this city-wide effort, we thought we didn't have the capacity or the expertise. We kept proposing ways we could engage in the short-term. Ways that would give them a yes but then allow us to go back to our regularly scheduled lives.

But God kept speaking and wouldn't let us off the hook. We sensed the call.

Caring for children and families in crisis is hard work. The children come from very difficult circumstances. Most of them have experienced deep levels of trauma that can surface when they finally feel safe in a new home. Many have special needs, whether it is academic or medical. The work is expensive. It is costly to help move a family or a child out of poverty. It takes a lot of patience and perseverance.

It's a lot easier to help at a distance, or just give up—not just with foster care but with many social issues.

THE NEED

The scale of injustice and human need today is staggering, both here and around the world:

- **Homelessness:** A total of 771,480 Americans experienced homelessness on a single night in 2024, the highest ever recorded.[3]
- **Poverty**: There are 36.8 million people living in poverty in this country. Which represents more than 1 in 10 Americans.[4]
- **Racial Disparities:** The median wealth of white, non-Hispanic households is ten times higher than that of black households, highlighting a significant racial wealth gap that has persisted for centuries.[5]
- **Slavery:** Globally, modern slavery affects an estimated 50 million people, with women and children being the most affected.[6]
- **Persecution:** 380 million Christians worldwide suffer high levels of persecution and discrimination for their faith. This is approximately 1 in 7 Christians globally.[7]

- **Abortion:** In 2024, more than 1 million abortions were performed in the United States, a number consistent with 2023 figures.[8] Globally, around 73 million induced abortions take place each year.[9]

These are not simply numbers. Each of these numbers has a name, each name has a story, and each story is precious to God. Suffering breaks the heart of God. It is not the way God designed us to live.

Yet, in the face of so much suffering, it can feel easier to withdraw. To pursue our own comfort. To cling to our security and stability.

It is difficult to witness the suffering in the world and still choose to engage.

THE POWER OF THE WORD

If we want to resist being co-opted by the world's political categories that tell us how to engage or not engage—and focus primarily on assigning blame for poverty—we must return to the foundation of our faith: the Word of God. It's not just our relationships with the poor that will make us less ideologically predictable—it's also our relationship with Scripture.

Research shows that regular Bible engagement makes people both more conservative and more liberal. For example, those who frequently read Scripture are more likely to oppose abortion and same-sex marriage—but are also more likely to support economic justice, racial equity, and care for the marginalized.[10] In other words, a biblical Christian should be growing in both personal holiness and public compassion. We were never meant to fit neatly into the categories offered to us by this world.

This isn't just about adults—it's especially true for the next generation. One study found that among college students, increased Bible reading was associated with greater commitment to Christian orthodoxy, deeper closeness to God, and increased civic engagement and altruism.[11] And the reverse is true as well: The less engaged we are with the Bible, the more passive we become—both in resisting moral compromise and in actively loving our neighbors.

Biblical justice begins not with political theory but with spiritual formation. It's not just about getting results. It's about love that costs something, truth that's always wrapped in grace, and mercy that points people back to the hope we have in Jesus. When justice flows from Scripture, it changes us before it changes the world.

THE LIE: CHARITY IS ENOUGH

The lie that most Christians believe today is that you can do justice with your spare change in your spare time. That charity is enough.

It's tempting to limit our engagement with those Jesus called "the least of these" to short-term relief efforts such as feeding the hungry at the soup kitchen, donating clothes to the homeless, or supporting disaster relief efforts. These are all good and biblical responses to immediate needs, but they fall into the category of charity work.

Justice, on the other hand, works toward long-term solutions by examining the systems that led to poverty in the first place.

There is a traditional proverb that states, "Give a man a fish, and he will eat for a day. Teach a man to fish, and he will eat for a lifetime." The goal is to move beyond short-term charity to community development where leaders are empowered to solve their own problems.

But justice asks the deeper question: What if they don't have access to a pond? Or even, Who owns the pond?

The lie that most Christians believe today is that you can do justice with your spare change in your spare time.

Ambassador Andrew Young, who served closely alongside Dr. Martin Luther King, Jr., often recalled how King challenged a charity-only approach. Young summarized King's repeated critique this way:

> I admire the Good Samaritan, but I don't want to be one. I am tired of picking up people along the Jericho Road. I am tired of seeing people battered and bruised and bloody, injured and jumped on, along the Jericho Roads of life. This road is dangerous. I don't want to pick up anyone else, along this Jericho Road; I want to fix the Jericho Road. I want to pave the Jericho Road, add street lights to the Jericho Road; make the Jericho Road safe for everybody.[12]

King was saying the whole road to Jericho must be transformed, for this is the sort of road that breeds robbers.

Or put another way, we can't keep pulling dead bodies out of the water. If we really care about those who are suffering, we must go upstream and see who is throwing them in.

Despite the urgent needs in our world today, justice has unfortunately become a polarizing topic in some churches. Some Christians adopt a charity-only approach to human suffering that fails to recognize systems of sin and injustice. Others take a systems-only approach, focusing on institutional sin while overlooking the sinfulness of the human heart.

The problem is, *neither side offers sacrifice.* One side serves, but then goes back to the comfort of their previously scheduled life.[13] The other side speaks about all the problems of the world but does not get personally involved.[14]

This leads both sides to believe the lie that we can do justice with our spare change in our spare time—to believe we can alleviate the suffering of the world in a way that doesn't cost us much. Just enough to alleviate our guilt, but not in a way that actually lifts someone out of poverty.

I live in a very politically progressive area where almost everyone pays lip service to address issues of poverty. The reality, though, is that few people actually know someone who is poor. Few people are walking in relationships with people who are poor. Most people think that if they just drive the right kind of car and vote a certain way, it will lead to the human flourishing we want to see.

We hide beyond our ideological frameworks that make us think we are making a difference, when in reality we are centering our own emotional comfort.

As Screwtape warns, "The more often he feels without acting, the less he will be able ever to act, and, in the long run, the less he will be able to feel."[15] True justice demands action, not passive emotion.

THE COUNTERFEIT IDENTITY: THE ARMCHAIR ACTIVIST

Believing the lie that you can change the world with your spare change in your spare time leads to the counterfeit identity of the Armchair Activist. An Armchair Activist is someone who expresses strong opinions about social, political, or humanitarian issues but takes little to no tangible action beyond online discussions, social media posts, or casual conversations.

Here are the key characteristics of an Armchair Activist:

- Engages in advocacy primarily from a *distance*—through tweets, shares, or online debates—rather than participating in direct action.
- Raises awareness but *avoids personal sacrifice* such as volunteering, donating, or physically participating in movements.
- *Criticizes* more than contributes, frequently calling out others' inaction while doing little themselves.
- *Lacks deep knowledge* of the issues they advocate for, relying on surface-level talking points from trending news and social media.

The Armchair Activist does not leave the comfort of their own home to engage in alleviating suffering. They can be described as a "slacktivist" or "performative activist." This is where someone presents outwardly that they are engaged—meaning they track the news and are able to stake out a clear position that comes across as compassionate toward the poor. But the reality is that there is no sacrifice or service involved.

Surprisingly, personal relationships with the poor make us less ideologically predictable. Though an Armchair Activist might succeed in raising awareness, true biblical justice demands far more. It requires commitment, sacrifice, and action—things that can't be accomplished from behind a screen or while sitting on a couch.

Armchair Activists often drift toward political extremes. Yet the sobering truth is this: Many couldn't get a letter of reference from a single person living in poverty, even if their lives depended on it.[16]

I mentioned this earlier but it bears repeating: Real relationships with the poor tend to shape us in complex ways—often making us both more conservative and more liberal. More conservative because of the bad choices, broken family systems, and personal irresponsibility that can perpetuate cycles of poverty. More liberal because of the systemic barriers, historic inequities, and limited opportunities that can stack the deck against someone's success.

But what happens when those relationships are absent, and we're shaped more by secular narratives than by Scripture or proximity to the poor?

We tend to reduce poverty to a moral failure—something that anyone could escape by just working harder or making better choices. We treat it as a character flaw rather than a complex reality shaped by generational inequities, broken systems, and spiritual warfare. So, we blame people and move on.

Or we swing to another extreme: We begin to see the world only in binary terms—everyone is either oppressed or an oppressor.

I remember a conversation with a college student who majored in sociology. He constantly heard messages that because he's a straight, white, Christian man, his opinions on injustice—especially about race, gender, or sexuality—automatically carried less weight. While he cared deeply about these issues, he felt like he had no role to play, since he was always "speaking from a place of privilege."

In this framework everyone is already sorted into fixed categories. The more marginalized identities a person holds—racial minority, female, LGBTQ+, disabled—the more moral authority they have. Their pain becomes proof of their righteousness.

And those from dominant groups, regardless of personal choices or character, are assumed to be complicit in oppression.

But this mindset misses the biblical story. Scripture doesn't assign guilt or innocence based on demographics. It calls every human being—regardless of race, gender, or status—to repentance, transformation, and reconciliation in Christ. The problem today isn't when we name injustice; it's allowing identity categories to replace the call to holiness and shared accountability before God.

The truth is that we are all sinners who fall short of the glory of God.[17] Which means we are all biased at some level and capable of prejudice and partiality. We are all oppressors at some level. But because some people have more power, they can inflict more damage than others. The common denominator in all our communities is this: Every human heart is deceitful and in need of God's transformative power.[18]

We need more credible voices in the public square who can offer a biblical vision for human flourishing—one that goes deeper than celebrating one's race, sex, or gender as central to our identity. The reality is that sin infects all people groups and will rear its ugly head no matter what our nationality or background.

The enemy is tricky and loves it when the church cannot properly define and articulate God's justice and righteousness. Without a common definition, we cannot appropriate this justice to the suffering we are witnessing in our world. The enemy loves this. He loves a silent church. A weak church. A divided church.

The enemy doesn't want the church caring about who Jesus calls "the least of these." He doesn't want the church gaining a moral voice in society through our sacrificial servant leadership. Satan knows if we fail to see Jesus in the eyes of the poor, then it will be a sign that those who claim to follow Christ don't really know Him.

For it was Jesus who said, "Truly I tell you, whatever you did for one of the least of these brothers and sisters of mine, you did for me" (Matthew 25:40).

A PRESIDENTIAL INVITATION

I was invited to meet with President Obama at the White House a few days after protests and riots broke out in Ferguson, Missouri, and then across the country in the wake of Michael Brown's shooting by police officer Darren Wilson.

I had a front-row seat to the tensest days of Obama's presidency as it related to his leadership on race in America. The streets were starting to burn in protest. What was the nation's first black president going to say and do in response? I sat next to Reverend Al Sharpton and Vice President Biden as we listened to some Ferguson youth share their pain, and we began to coordinate with the police chiefs there on a response that could help communities feel safe again.

When I met President Obama, he shared how he knew about our ministry DC127 and thanked me for my work with foster children in D.C. He invited me to follow up from the meeting and share my thoughts of how we could move forward as a country in response to these race riots and the ongoing breakdown in trust between the community and cops. He wanted to specifically hear what I thought the faith community could do in response.

Here is an excerpt from the letter I wrote to him:

> The vision for reconciliation must go deeper than the ones currently being offered today. Too often, when

> faith is talked about in the political or legislative context, it is used instrumentally. Faith becomes a means to an end, and in this case, justice or inclusion being the highest goal or end. The problem is when the vision for reconciliation is limited to "diversity" or "inclusion" alone, it does not go far enough. It easily becomes another way groups contend for more power, failing to offer a vision any higher than promoting one's own ethnicity, gender, or culture as the end in itself.
>
> Instead, we need to speak to the hearts and minds of people by casting a vision of who we are called to be as a people, and seeing reconciliation as a means to that larger vision. Shared sacrifice will be made when we rise above the current polarizations and are given a vision of reconciliation that is worth giving our entire lives to.

That meeting—and others like it—showed me just how crucial it is that the church reclaims its prophetic voice. But in doing so, we must not trade biblical conviction for cultural conformity. If our message simply echoes the world's categories, we lose the very power that makes reconciliation possible.

THE CULTURAL CONFUSION: JUSTICE GETS HIJACKED

The Ferguson protests and their aftermath was the beginning of the rise of "identity politics" in America—where one's self-defined identity around whatever "status" began to be framed in "salvific terms." For example, a young activist might say, "My journey as a queer woman of color *is* my truth. This is how I've found freedom." In this framework, salvation isn't found in Christ but in discovering and expressing one's identity—and liberation from oppression becomes the highest good.

While progressives rightly identified many of the historic injustices that were continuing to manifest to this day, their solutions to the problems were often more rooted in secular ideology than a Christian worldview.

That left evangelicals like myself, who were known for our decades of advocacy for the poor, a bit homeless politically. While we were extremely committed to building a more just and equal society, the leadership of the emerging Black Lives Matter movement and of the continuing LGBTQ+ movement (gay marriage would be legalized a few months later in June 2015 with the *Obergefell v. Hodges* Supreme Court decision) was becoming more and more secular.

Historically social movements in America have been rooted in the church (abolition of slavery, child suffrage, women's suffrage, civil rights). The leaders of these movements were church leaders who were biblically orthodox and helped disciple the masses that it is not enough to "win" on an issue if you become less faithful as a follower of Jesus in the process. They learned how to guide the church to be in but not of the world as they engaged in the important work of justice.

We are now confronted with major social ills in our nation and world, and yet the church is not spiritually formed to respond. Pastors are rarely seen as trusted voices in society, and Christians are often viewed as part of the problem. Not only do we find ourselves alienated from an increasingly secular society, but we have a hard time finding common ground within an increasingly secularized *church*.

For centuries in America, you could assume that most Christians were Bible believing. Meaning, they believed in salvation through Christ alone, the authority of Scripture, and a biblical view of marriage and family. Therefore, when it came to responding to the needs of the poor and suffering, leaders could draw upon these common values and beliefs to mobilize people to action.

This is no longer the case. Today, there is no consensus, even among major denominations, around these core doctrines. As a result, the church is not united in its witness to an unbelieving world. This becomes even more challenging when you see the increasing numbers who are no longer active in church.

Into this void step polarizing politics and secular voices that *redefine justice in unbiblical and non-sacrificial terms.*

Justice is getting hijacked. We are letting the world come into the church, rather than the church going into the world.

SOCIAL JUSTICE VS. BIBLICAL JUSTICE

Dr. King's commitment to social change was rooted in a vision of the kingdom of God—one that didn't stop with changing laws but called for changed hearts. That's why, even after the Civil Rights Act and Voting Rights Act were passed, he kept marching on. For King, true justice meant reconciliation, not just integration.

The same was true for Archbishop Desmond Tutu. After the fall of apartheid in South Africa, he didn't just celebrate a political victory. He set up the Truth and Reconciliation Commission—not to exact revenge, but to pursue forgiveness. This became a model for nations all over the world of the deeper work of biblical justice. Tutu understood that structural change must be accompanied by heart change. That's biblical justice.

However, many Christians think social justice and biblical justice are the same thing.

It is not enough to "win" on an issue if you become less faithful as a follower of Jesus in the process.

Many secular movements are motivated by a sincere desire to right wrongs and relieve suffering—and in that, they reflect something of God's heart, even if they lack the full story.

Social justice is about treating people equally and ensuring everyone has a fair chance. It seeks to uphold basic human dignity at the societal level and often addresses urgent needs and systemic wrongs. That's good and necessary work—and in many cases, Christians should gladly participate.

But biblical justice calls us much deeper. It not only seeks to restore systems—it seeks to restore people. It addresses not just what's broken *around* us, but also what's broken *within* us. It roots our pursuit of justice in God's character, in eternal truth, and in a vision of heaven breaking into earth. It holds together righteousness and mercy, repentance and reconciliation, love of neighbor and worship of God.

Where social justice often stops at fairness, biblical justice pushes us toward transformation. It invites us not just to fix the world but to be changed ourselves.

Jesus gave us the clearest definition of biblical justice when He taught us to pray, "Your kingdom come, your will be done, on earth as it is in heaven."[19] Biblical justice begins with that vision of heaven—and brings it to bear on earth.

Social justice is a partial expression of the fuller justice God desires. But biblical justice goes further—restoring not only systems, but also hearts, relationships, and our standing before God.

Biblical justice gives eternal perspective to the work we've been called to here on earth. It doesn't dismiss the need for structural change, but it roots our action in a vision of God's kingdom, not just human progress. It begins with heaven and then reshapes how we live on earth.

As C. S. Lewis writes, "Aim at heaven and you will get earth 'thrown in.' Aim at earth and you will get neither."[20]

God's vision for justice is not simply a legal one, rooted in the laws of man. God's vision for justice is also about right relationships.

Which is why when we are committed to biblical justice it is not enough to just win an election or win on our issue in a campaign. We must also become more faithful followers of Jesus in the process.

As Christians we must learn to play the long game where worship and justice come together. Jesus and justice come together. Biblical engagement and justice come together. Local church community and justice come together.

By contrast, secular culture wants the fruits of justice without the roots. It wants the fruit of a more just and equitable society, something where we as the church should share common ground. But the temptation for the church is to water down our beliefs in our efforts to build partnerships for justice. If we are not careful, we can easily lose our distinct beliefs that lead to sacrificial justice in the first place.

In my experience, the world will gladly receive our funding and volunteers—the question is whether we will maintain our distinct witness and beliefs as we engage with secular justice movements. I believe it is better for us to be clear about our biblical convictions so that we don't allow justice to get redefined for our people in unhelpful humanistic ways.

The tendency is to center humanity over and above God. But once the authority of God has been rejected, there is no common definition of justice. And this is where it gets very dangerous because then there can be no accountability to a higher power or eternal truth who defines what is right and wrong. Everything becomes subjective and left up to personal interpretation. And as a result, the poor are always those who lose the most in the end.

Churches today seem confused about the work of justice. They are either on the sidelines, believing that charity is enough, or they have a vision of justice that is more politically partisan than it is biblically faithful. That is more influenced by secular media than it is by the Word of God.

This is why it is so important to have conversations about justice in the local church. One way our church does this is by creating spaces for us to listen to one another's stories with different heritage month events and workshops throughout the year. With over eighty nations represented in our church, we each have unique stories to share. When these spaces are anchored in biblical teaching, God's vision of justice is upheld, and the church becomes a place where hard conversations don't divide us but disciple us.

It is from the local church that we can then offer society a fresh vision of what heaven could look like here on earth, a vision that can change not only laws but human hearts.

THE TRUTH: PRIORITY FOR THE POOR

The lie that charity is enough confronts us with the questions, What do I really believe about the poor? Do I have any responsibility toward them?

The Bible presents an unmistakable priority for the poor. On page after page it talks about money and possessions as well as the poor, the widow, and the stranger. In fact, one way to assess the spiritual temperature of an individual or even a nation is to test how they care for the most vulnerable.

Our calling as Christians is to move toward the suffering of the world just as Christ moved toward us. To spend less time trying to *explain* people's suffering (as Job's friends did), and instead seek to *identify* with people's pain, as Jesus does with ours.

We see God's priority for the poor throughout the Bible.

We see it in the Law. In Exodus, God told the Israelites to not oppress the foreigners, reminding them they were foreigners in Egypt. To not take advantage of the widow or fatherless.[21] In Leviticus, God told his people to leave the edges of the harvest in their fields for the poor and foreigners.[22] In Deuteronomy, He commanded His people to not take advantage of the hired worker who is poor and needy.[23]

The most dominant theme of the Old Testament is God's covenantal relationship with His people—marked by His steadfast love, their call to faithfulness, and His unfolding plan of redemption. The greatest threat to that love is idolatry. God clearly states in the first of the Ten Commandments, "You shall have no other gods before me."[24] And then in the second commandment, "You shall not make for yourself an image in the form of anything in heaven above or on the earth beneath or in the waters below. You shall not bow down to them or worship them."[25]

Furthermore, the Old Testament attests that wherever you have idolatry you are likely to see oppression of the poor. False worship leads to a breakdown of moral order, where power and wealth become ultimate gods. As a result, the poor are neglected, exploited, and silenced. This idolatry then puts humanity in the driver's seat and normalizes using power for personal benefit rather than in love of neighbor.

Justice has always been on God's heart. Exodus tells the

story of the Israelites crying out to God after hundreds of years of slavery. Before Moses turned up on the scene to respond to the call to confront Pharaoh and lead the Israelites out of slavery, God made it clear: "I have indeed seen the misery of my people in Egypt. I have heard them crying out because of their slave drivers, and I am concerned about their suffering."[26]

We hear God's priority for the poor in the Prophets. Isaiah told us to "do right; seek justice. Defend the oppressed. Take up the cause of the fatherless; plead the case of the widow."[27] He called for the kind of fast that looses the chains of injustice and leads to sharing our food with the hungry.[28] Amos called for the kind of justice that rolls down like a river, and for righteousness that flows like an ever-flowing stream.[29] Micah famously summarized the whole Law and Prophets by saying, "What does the LORD require of you? To act justly and to love mercy and to walk humbly with your God."[30]

We hear God's priority for the poor in the Psalms. Calling us to rescue the weak and the needy and deliver them from the hand of the wicked.[31] King Solomon warned us that "whoever oppresses the poor shows contempt for their Maker, but whoever is kind to the needy honors God."[32] Proverbs commands us to "speak up for those who cannot speak for themselves [and] defend the rights of the poor and needy."[33]

We hear a priority for the poor featured in Jesus' life and teachings. He quoted Isaiah 61 as he began his public ministry, saying the Spirit of the Lord was upon Him, to preach good news to *the poor.*[34] He declared the poor as "blessed" in the Beatitudes, affirming their value and dignity in contrast to how society viewed them.[35] He shared about the Good Samaritan, warning us not to forget the inseparable link between faith and action.[36] He commanded the rich young ruler to first sell everything he had and give to the poor in order to follow Jesus and experience the true treasures of heaven.[37] Paul even said that though Jesus was rich, for our sakes He became poor.[38] In fact, Jesus himself said He had nowhere to lay his head.[39]

We hear this priority for the poor in the early church. They sold their possessions and gave to anyone who had need.[40] It says a few chapters later that the result was "there were no needy persons among them."[41] The early church raised up new leaders to ensure the widows were cared for and fed as the church grew and put constraints on the apostles' time.[42]

We hear this priority for the poor in the Epistles. When the apostles sent Paul to bring the gospel to the Gentiles, they pleaded that he should continue to remember the poor, something Paul was eager to keep doing.[43] In his epistle, John questioned if someone can claim authentic Christian faith if they have the means to help a brother in need but refuse.[44]

God's priority for the poor is all over the Bible. In fact, the American Bible Society created *The Poverty & Justice Bible* that literally highlights more than two thousand verses that are meant to wake us up to issues of poverty and justice.[45]

A PERSONAL AWAKENING: BABY MASA

Human suffering is something I had to learn to confront at a young age. My parents moved to Liberia to serve as missionaries when I was six years old.

One of the things that made a strong impression on me was the depth of poverty. I had never gone without a meal, so it really surprised me.

My dad would often take me to the remote villages on Saturdays to serve with him. I remember there was a baby named Masa who was about a year old who was born malnourished. She was literally skin and bones. Whenever we would take her an egg or protein she would progress and gain weight. Whenever we didn't make that three-mile hike on Saturdays, she regressed.

Sadly, this little girl ended up dying of hunger. It haunted me. It still haunts me. How do we allow so many children to die each day of completely preventable causes?

This early encounter with suffering showed me the high cost of disengagement—and the potential of the church to meet suffering with real presence and lasting hope.

Twenty years ago, nearly thirty thousand children under the age of five died each day from preventable causes such as diarrhea, malaria, and malnutrition. Today that number has been dramatically reduced to 13,100 per day.[46] This massive decrease is evidence of what's possible when churches, foundations, and governments work together to provide clean water, maternal care, vaccines, and nutrition. These are not abstract initiatives—they save lives. And what makes this more remarkable is that this progress happened while our global population grew by more than two billion people.[47]

Much of this success was made possible because Christians stepped up—advocating, giving, serving, and building partnerships across sectors. While faith-based organizations have been at the forefront of global development, we must recognize that the scale of human suffering exceeds what Christians alone can alleviate. Government carries a God-ordained responsibility to restrain evil and promote justice.[48]

Governments and secular institutions will never reflect the full biblical justice we are called to embody in the church—but that doesn't make their role insignificant. Efforts such as international aid and access to healthcare literally save lives. As Christians, we should affirm the doctrine of common grace: that God, in His mercy, works through all people to accomplish good.

THE CRISIS OF SECULAR JUSTICE

Affirming God's work through secular institutions doesn't mean we should uncritically adopt their methods or message. This requires discernment, because many models for moving beyond charity toward justice are increasingly shaped by secular ideologies.

Too often, these movements are rooted *more in outer agitation than inner formation,* producing people who are angry, divided, and spiritually unrooted. Allegiance shifts from God to political platforms.[49]

They offer salvation-like promises, but fail to acknowledge human depravity or provide a path to redemption. History shows that without a school of spiritual formation, such as the local church, the oppressed often become the next oppressors. Without discipleship there is no urgency—or process—for forgiveness, reconciliation, and unity.

Secular justice fosters resentment and blame more than healing. It breeds a victim mentality, where the problem is always outside the room, never within. It oversimplifies complex human relationships and ignores individual agency.

Though often well-intentioned, the messages of secular justice movements are ultimately insufficient. When imported into the church, they strip the gospel of its saving power—deconstructing Christ as the only path to salvation and undermining the authority of Scripture in the name of doing the "real" work of justice.

Once again, if the church doesn't disciple its people, the world gladly will. The world will teach us to avoid relational responsibility and hide behind political ideology to justify our indifference.

As David Brooks observes, "To be moral in this world, you don't have to feed the hungry or sit with the widow. You just have to be liberal or conservative, you just have to feel properly enraged at the people you find contemptible."[50]

Political engagement is an important responsibility—but it cannot replace Christian community, spiritual formation, or walking in solidarity with the poor. Only the gospel can form people who love sacrificially and serve consistently.

THE COMMITMENT: SOLIDARITY WITH THE POOR (BIBLICAL JUSTICE)

Generosity and solidarity are never one-way gifts. When we step into the lives of those who are struggling, it meets real needs—but it also reorients our hearts toward God's kingdom. We begin to see the world differently. We begin to see *people* differently. And most important, we begin to see Christ in unexpected places.

Jesus said, "'For I was hungry and you gave me something to eat, I was thirsty and you gave me something to drink, I was a stranger and you invited me in, I needed clothes and you clothed me, I was sick and you looked after me, I was in prison and you came to visit me . . . Truly I tell you, whatever you did for one of the least of these brothers and sisters of mine, you did for me'" (Matthew 25:35–36, 40).

Jesus invites us to *see Him* in the face of the poor. Not just to serve, but to build relationships. To welcome the stranger. To share a meal. To offer presence. When we do this, we are not simply helping another human being—we are ministering to *Christ*.

And this isn't an isolated command. It's deeply connected to everything else we've talked about in this book. When you start to believe it's all about you, you withdraw from community, compartmentalize your faith, and disengage from Scripture. These lies don't just harm your spiritual life—they also harden your heart toward the needs around you. The effects of idolatry are devastating, both for our souls and for the poor in our communities.

Here's the truth: It starts with God. His plan for transformation flows through the church. Jesus is Lord over every part of our lives—not just our beliefs, but our actions. The Bible is God's authoritative Word, shaping how we see justice. And from beginning to end, God's heart beats for the poor.

When we believe any one of these cultural lies, it can undo our spiritual formation across multiple areas. That's why we must stay alert. The enemy seeks to undermine our commitment to justice by pushing us toward political commentary rather than relational responsibility—toward ideological rage instead of Spirit-led compassion. Toward explaining people's suffering instead of being present with people *in* their suffering.

John Wesley, the founder of the Methodist movement, once said that we should carry relief to the poor rather than send it. It may be more efficient for us to donate online, but God calls us to *personally deliver* what is needed, whenever we can. This is for our sake and for the sake of the poor.[51] Wesley considered regular visitation of the poor as essential for Christian discipleship, just like prayer and communion.[52]

Jesus invites us to see Him in the face of the poor.

But in our efforts to engage, we have to be careful not to bring an "activist" spirit into these relationships. Jesus never told us to fix our neighbor, but rather to *love* our neighbor. And love takes time. It grows through empathy, compassion, and presence. It requires more than money—it requires margin. It asks for our availability. Our patience. Our willingness to slow down and truly *listen*.

And if we do slow down, we'll hear stories of suffering that are far deeper than we imagined. Stories that break our heart and leave us unsure of what to say. Often, there *is* nothing to say—only our presence and our prayers. But it's in those very moments that we begin to "see Christ in the distressing disguise of the poor."[53]

That's the mystery of solidarity: When you leave your comfort zone to be with someone in their suffering, Christ meets you there. And often, you'll find that the one you came to serve ends up ministering to you. Their faith. Their peace. Their gratitude. Their perspective. It convicts you. It humbles you. It awakens something in your spirit that comfort and convenience never could.

MOVING FORWARD

So, let me ask you: Who has God placed in your life that you need to slow down and pay more attention to? Is there someone on the margins He's inviting you to befriend? Is there an organization in your city that doesn't just serve the poor, but builds friendships? That's where the invitation begins. Not in charity. In relationship.

And just like the other commitments in this book—restoring true worship, investing in the church, surrendering to the lordship of Jesus, engaging daily with Scripture—this one flows from the same place. They're all connected. Without those first four, this fifth commitment to justice can become distorted. You may look engaged online. You may sound informed in conversation. But your actual life remains unchanged.

You might become an Armchair Activist, expressing strong opinions, getting recognition for your "wokeness" or "charity," but lacking the tangible, sacrificial love Jesus modeled. Without deep spiritual formation, justice becomes just another performance. But when justice flows from worship, discipleship, surrender, and Scripture, it becomes a way of life.

Justice must be rooted in biblical truth, not secular ideologies or partisan agendas. It must be personal, not just political. And it must be costly—demanding more than our words or donations. It requires our presence, our time, and our lives.

God's call is clear: Move beyond charity and pursue biblical justice. Build real friendships with the poor. Resist the drift toward performative activism. Reject the lie that justice is optional or effortless. The enemy wants a silent, disengaged church. But Jesus calls us to see Him in the faces of the least of these.

I still think about baby Masa. Her story reminds me that this isn't theoretical. If we truly believe what Jesus said in Matthew 25, then every act of compassion becomes sacred. Every visit, every meal, every step toward someone in need is a step toward Christ Himself.

So where do we find the power to live this way? Not in strategy. Not in guilt. But in truth and power. And that's exactly where we go next—by confronting another dangerous lie Christians are tempted to believe.

DISCUSSION AND REFLECTION QUESTIONS

Lie 5: Charity Is Enough

1. **The Armchair Activist**

   In what ways have you seen "armchair activism" manifest in your own life or the lives of those around you? How does this compare to biblical justice?

2. **Charity vs. Justice**

   How does the distinction between charity (short-term relief) and justice (long-term transformation) change your perspective on how to serve the poor and marginalized?

3. **The Cost of Biblical Justice**

   Justice requires more than spare change and spare time. How does sacrificial justice challenge the way you currently engage with issues of poverty, race, and injustice?

4. **Seeing Christ in the Poor**

   Jesus said in Matthew 25:40, "Whatever you did for one of the least of these brothers and sisters of mine, you did for me." How does this verse shape your view of justice and your personal responsibility to the poor?

5. **The Role of the Local Church**

   What role should the local church play in addressing injustice? How does your church currently engage, and what are some ways it could deepen its commitment?

6. **Moving Beyond Political Ideologies**

   How does secular political ideology (whether conservative or progressive) shape or distort your approach to justice? How can you ensure your justice efforts are biblically grounded more than politically partisan?

7. **Personal Relationships with the Poor**

   Do you personally know someone living in poverty? If not, what are some intentional steps you can take to build relationships with those in need?

8. **Worship and Justice**

   How does worship (both private and corporate) fuel a commitment to justice? What are the pitfalls to pursuing justice apart from a deep relationship with Christ?

9. **The Enemy's Strategy**

   The enemy loves it when Christians are disengaged from justice or when justice is redefined in secular terms. How have you seen this strategy play out in churches or in culture?

10. **A Personal Next Step**

    What is one concrete step you can take this week to move beyond charity and step into biblical justice in your community?

6

WHEN REASON REPLACES REVELATION

From Rational Skepticism to Spirit-Filled Power

When the humans disbelieve in our existence we lose all the pleasing results . . . On the other hand, when they believe in us, we cannot make them materialists and skeptics.

—*The Screwtape Letters,* Letter 7

I was ten years old the first time I feared for my life.

My family was living in Kuwait as missionaries during the Persian Gulf War when Saddam Hussein's forces invaded. We were taken hostage.

It was terrifying. My mom, my brother, and I were released after six weeks, but my dad remained a hostage for another three months.

People around the world were praying for his release—literally millions. During a specific week when churches had been especially mobilized to pray, something extraordinary happened. Saddam Hussein began having disturbing dreams—so intense that he couldn't sleep. He later said that *God was troubling his spirit.*

At the time, Saddam had taken hostages from Western countries and placed them at military sites across Iraq and Kuwait to use as human shields. It was his last remaining tactic to prevent an invasion of over 500,000 U.S. troops who were waiting in Saudi Arabia. But after these sleepless nights from troubling dreams, Saddam shocked his cabinet by ordering the release of the hostages. The next day, my dad was on a plane back to the United States.

> This lie is when the head and heart move in different directions.

Even years later, former Secretary of State James Baker and other senior officials couldn't explain why Hussein made that decision. My dad had the opportunity to speak with President George H. W. Bush, who told him plainly: "I still do not know why Hussein released the hostages. But it made the decision to invade Kuwait much easier."

He didn't know. But I do. It was God. It was God who woke Saddam up. God who troubled his spirit. God who moved on the heart of one of the world's most wicked leaders in response to the prayers of His people.

There is no rational explanation for it. But that's the point. Some things are simply supernatural.

I grew up Baptist, firmly planted in the "truth" camp. The joke was: *We believe in the Father, the Son, and the Holy Bible.*

The third member of the Trinity? He's only mentioned in the context of bringing us to salvation, not for supernatural empowerment for life and ministry. We were taught about the service gifts—leadership, hospitality, generosity—but not the supernatural gifts of healing, tongues, and prophecy, or in signs and wonders.

I am deeply grateful for my Baptist roots and the strong biblical foundation I received. But I also long to experience the fullness of everything God has for us.

Our culture conditions us to value education over supernatural empowerment, understanding over mystery, and logic over faith. I see it daily here in Washington, D.C., which consistently ranks as the most educated city in the country.[1] This mindset can serve us well in the classroom or the boardroom. But when brought before God, it becomes a liability. It teaches us to believe *only* what we can explain, and in doing so, cuts us off from the very power we need the most.

THE LIE: EVERYTHING IS RATIONAL

The sixth lie that many Christians believe is this: *Everything is rational*—that I must fully understand something in order to believe it.

This is the lie that causes the head and the heart to move in different directions. It reduces worship to truth without Spirit and doctrine to belief without dependence.[2]

Like all the best lies, this one is rooted in a half-truth.

Yes, we are called to love God with all our minds.[3]

Yes, we are to worship in Spirit and in truth.[4]

Yes, learning is a lifelong journey, and we should get all the education we can.[5]

But here is where the lie creeps in: We start to believe that everything about God must be explainable to be true.

Our culture conditions us to value education over supernatural empowerment, understanding over mystery, and logic over faith.

But faith doesn't have to be fully logical and comprehensible to be valid.

Paul challenged this assumption in his letter to the Corinthians. Quoting Isaiah 64:4, he wrote: "'What no eye has seen, what no ear has heard, and what no human mind has conceived'—the things God has prepared for those who love him—these are the things God has revealed to us by his Spirit" (1 Corinthians 2:9–10).

When we depend more on logic than revelation, we begin to limit God to our own understanding.[6]

But what if God still works in ways that defy human explanation?

Let me share one more story.

My best friend, Chris, is a committed Christian and a successful entrepreneur. When his therapist had to cancel upcoming appointments due to a recent lung cancer diagnosis, she told him she'd be undergoing surgery the following week. Before she left, Chris simply asked, "Can I pray for you?"

A week later, the surgery never happened.

A new scan revealed that the tumor had calcified and completely encapsulated itself within that week. No surgery was needed. The chief of pulmonology asked her, "Are you a praying woman?" He said he had seen something like this happen only once before in his career.

She later told Chris what had happened. She remembered how, during his simple prayer, her legs and feet had started burning. At the time, she didn't understand it. But looking back, she knew—that was when the healing took place.

Chris's prayer wasn't flashy. It wasn't loud or dramatic. It was just obedient. He agreed with heaven for her healing—and God moved.

RATIONALISM: THE ROOT OF THE LIE

The idea that we must fully understand something in order to believe it is rooted in rationalism. This is the belief that human reason is the ultimate and most reliable source of truth. Rationalism elevates logic, intellect, and empirical evidence above all else, often dismissing faith, emotion, tradition, and divine revelation as unreliable or inferior ways of knowing.

This way of thinking emerged powerfully during the Enlightenment, when philosophers began to believe that reason alone could unlock every mystery of the universe and solve every human problem.

Used rightly, rational thought is a powerful gift. It's something to be stewarded well—especially when defending our faith through apologetics or discerning truth from error. But when rationalism becomes a *worldview,* it leads to a dangerous reductionism. It trains us to trust only what we can see, measure, and prove. It denies the validity of mystery, the possibility of miracles, and the presence of the supernatural.

Rationalism reduces God from a living, personal Being to an abstract concept or distant force. It treats faith as irrational, devotion as primitive, and divine revelation as suspect.

Paul encountered this mindset in Corinth, where Greek philosophers prided themselves on intellectual sophistication and rhetorical skill. But he boldly declared, "The foolishness of God is wiser than human wisdom, and the weakness of God is stronger than human strength" (1 Corinthians 1:25).

God does not ask us to check our minds at the door of the church—but neither does He ask us to limit our worship to what we can fully comprehend. Faith invites us into mystery—not away from thought, but beyond it.

In our church, there is a couple who embodies this tension

beautifully. Between the two of them, they have Ivy League degrees, doctorate degrees, and a medical degree. They serve in Washington, D.C., working to develop strategies to promote international development.

Together, they've refused to let their academic credentials become a ceiling for their faith. As licensed ministers of the gospel, they lead a ministry that equips people to pray with authority and contend for revival in the midst of our nation's capital. They are living proof that being smart doesn't mean being spiritually skeptical—and that being filled with the Spirit doesn't mean abandoning reason.

I've met so many Christians—especially in highly educated circles—who deeply love Jesus but struggle to embrace anything that feels "too supernatural." They're afraid of being labeled irrational or weird. But in their fear of excess, they often end up with a faith that feels safe but is powerless.

Paul asked the Corinthians, "Who has known the mind of the Lord so as to instruct him?"[7] Then he answered with astonishing confidence: "But we have the mind of Christ."[8]

In other words, by the Spirit, we grow into the wisdom and likeness of Christ—where intellectual depth and spiritual intimacy are no longer at odds.

The problem arises when pride turns our faith into a research project—when we treat God like a subject to be studied rather than a Person to be loved and obeyed.

The pride of rationalism says, "I must understand before I obey." It exalts human reason as the highest source of truth. But it fails to account that some things are simply revealed by the Spirit.[9]

When rationalism gets a foothold in our minds, we begin to miss out on the fullness of God. We trade wonder for control. We become vulnerable to hollow and deceptive philosophies that sound intelligent but are ultimately powerless to save.[10]

WHEN RATIONALISM REPLACES FAITH

The danger of rationalism is not just that it dismisses faith but that it seeks to *replace* faith altogether. It becomes an overarching worldview, redefining what is considered real or true. And it often gives rise to two deeply influential distortions in our modern world.

The first is what some call *scientism*—the belief that science alone can provide truth. Now, science is a gift from God. It helps us understand creation, cure diseases, and improve life on earth. But scientism elevates science from a method of inquiry to a worldview of supremacy. It dismisses theology, morality, and spiritual experience as irrelevant or inferior—because they can't be tested in a lab.

But as Paul reminded us in Colossians 1:16, "All things were created through Him and for Him" (NKJV). Science can help us explore God's world, but it does not define it. Reality is not limited to what can be measured. God is the ultimate source and sustainer of all things—seen and unseen.

A second distortion that flows from rationalism is *materialism*—the belief that only the physical world is real. This doesn't just deny miracles; it denies the soul, the afterlife, and the entire supernatural realm. It reduces human beings to what can be seen, touched, or measured.

In the church, we often think of materialism as the love of money or possessions. But this is even more deceptive. This form of materialism undermines the soul itself. It strips away meaning, purpose, and eternity.

And tragically, many people today aren't rejecting God because they've reasoned Him away; instead they've been taught He was never there to begin with. That the material world is all there is. That faith is irrational because it cannot be tested, tracked, or proven.

But Scripture speaks directly to this. Paul wrote, "So we fix our eyes not on what is seen, but on what is unseen. For what is seen is temporary, but what is unseen is eternal" (2 Corinthians 4:18).

That's why rationalism—and the distortions it spawns—is so deceptive. It packages itself as intellectual progress, but it ultimately leads us to reject mystery, miracles, and the supernatural.

Rationalism says, "Only reason and logic determine truth."

Scientism says, "Only what science can measure is real."

Materialism says, "If we can't detect it physically, it doesn't exist."

This is the opposite of walking by faith.

In our culture today, faith is often dismissed as something for the uneducated, the uninformed, or the emotionally weak. People say things like "I believe in facts, not faith," or "That's fine if religion helps you—but I need something real."

But Scripture tells a different story. The struggle is not *faith versus reason.* It's *faith versus unbelief.* Between those who take God at His word, and those who insist on creating their own truth.

If you buy into the lie that you must fully understand before you can believe, you will gradually lose your capacity for wonder, your openness to the miraculous, and ultimately, your connection to the living God.

This mindset doesn't always lead to outright atheism. More often, it creates a more subtle spiritual condition—what I call the *skeptical believer.*

THE COUNTERFEIT IDENTITY: THE SKEPTICAL BELIEVER

A Skeptical Believer is someone who identifies as a Christian but struggles with doubt, filtering their faith through constant questioning, analysis, and intellectual scrutiny. In fact, doubt is no longer something they wrestle with—it's something they've come to center their identity around.

A Skeptical Believer tends to:

- Dismiss miracles as coincidences.
- Ignore spiritual warfare.
- Doubt heaven and hell because they don't seem rational.

This isn't just a problem outside of the church (think Richard Dawkins or Sam Harris). It's increasingly creeping into the church itself—and it often goes undetected until it is too late.

What may begin as normal human doubt or a desire for intellectual integrity slowly morphs into something more dangerous: an identity built around skepticism, uncertainty, and eventually unbelief.

A skeptical believer is someone who identifies as a Christian but struggles with doubt, filtering their faith through constant questioning, analysis, and intellectual scrutiny.

This is how it often happens: You are raised in the church with a fairly orthodox Christian worldview—meaning you believe the Bible and the core teachings that Christians have held for centuries. But as you leave home and step into broader social life and your university studies, you encounter a world where skepticism toward faith is the norm. And without realizing it, you start to absorb that perspective. You begin to see skepticism not just as normal, but as mature.

At first, you still see value in the church—not necessarily because you share its beliefs, but because you enjoy its community and social impact. So, you stay involved, not out of conviction, but for connection. You understand the culture of a church enough to know how to fit in and get your social needs met. You are discerning enough to know what questions you can raise and which ones are best kept to yourself.

Externally things look much the same, yet internally something has shifted. Something theological. And if you are honest, you no longer truly believe the gospel. That God sent His one and only Son into this world to reconcile you as a sinner to a holy God.

You're doing well. Upwardly mobile. Fitting in with the mainstream culture. You have career prospects, dating options, influence. Why bother with religion? It feels like more of a barrier than a blessing.

It's at this point that the identity of the skeptical believer has taken hold.

Let's be clear: Having doubts is not the issue. Scripture gives space for doubt. "I believe; help my unbelief" (Mark 9:24, NKJV) is the desperate cry of a father seeking Jesus to heal his son. The problem isn't the presence of questions—it's when doubt becomes the *center* of your faith, rather than a pathway toward deeper trust in God.

You'll know when skepticism has taken root when your questions dominate every spiritual conversation. Small groups stop pursuing truth and start normalizing uncertainty. The goal shifts from seeking answers to endlessly questioning everything. The more these doubts are shared, the more they become a badge of intellectual depth. And those who hold fast to biblical convictions? They start fading into the background.

It feels justified—because your doubts mirror the mindset of your non-believing friends. You hope that by creating a church culture that welcomes questioning, your friends might feel more comfortable attending. But they rarely do. And even when they do, they rarely encounter a clear call to repentance.

Eventually, skepticism isn't just tolerated—it's celebrated. Doubt is no longer a phase on the way to faith. It becomes a virtue in and of itself.

And because this way of thinking is so deeply ingrained in secular culture, it rarely gets challenged. You don't notice it in yourself. And often, neither does the church. But the result is that a fully secularized worldview begins to take root within the body of Christ—not as an outside attack, but as an internal drift.

We often think of skepticism as something that keeps people from coming to faith. But it just as easily infects those who have *already* come to faith—shaping their discipleship journey around uncertainty rather than trust.

Because the Skeptical Believer often sounds intelligent, their influence can be outsized. Even church leadership may hesitate to lovingly challenge this mindset for fear of sounding anti-intellectual. But left unchecked, this posture begins to normalize a secular worldview within the church itself.

The question is: Will we recognize it before it takes root—in our churches and in our own hearts?

GNOSTICISM: THE ANCIENT HERESY BEHIND MODERN SKEPTICISM

Long before post-Enlightenment rationalism, the early church battled a similar heresy: Gnosticism.

Gnosticism redefined salvation as something attained through secret knowledge (*gnosis*) rather than faith in Christ. Like rationalism today, it prioritized human wisdom over God's Word and distorted the heart of the gospel. Gnostics downplayed the physical world, elevating intellectual enlightenment and spiritual mysticism over the embodied reality of Christ's incarnation.

The early church confronted a developing form of Gnosticism, which promoted a dualistic worldview—the belief that the material world was inherently evil or corrupt, while the spiritual realm alone was pure and good. Many Gnostics even taught that the physical world was created by a lower, corrupt being—separate from the supreme, unknowable God.

One of Gnosticism's most dangerous distortions was its denial of Christ's incarnation and humanity. To them, Jesus only *appeared* to have a physical body. This is why John wrote a direct warning: "Many deceivers, who do not acknowledge Jesus Christ as coming in the flesh, have gone out into the world. Any such person is the deceiver and the antichrist" (2 John v. 7).

While Gnosticism was a radical departure from early Christianity, it remains a cautionary example of how the gospel can be distorted. Its core errors continue today through modern rationalism and materialism.

Today materialists argue that only the physical world exists, rejecting any spiritual reality. Rationalists demand that faith must be fully explainable and logical, dismissing mystery or miracles altogether. Both in their own way say, "If I can't see it, touch it, measure it, it isn't real."

But the Bible paints a very different picture:

- **Faith is rooted in both the physical and the spiritual.** "The Word became flesh and made his dwelling among us. We have seen his glory" (John 1:14). Jesus was fully God and fully man, proving that the physical world is not evil but an essential part of God's creation and redemption.
- **The supernatural is just as real as the material.** "So we fix our eyes not on what is seen, but on what is unseen, since what is seen is temporary, but what is unseen is eternal" (2 Corinthians 4:18). The material world is not ultimate, but neither is it meaningless. The unseen realm is just as real.
- **True wisdom comes from God and not from human intellect alone.** "The fear of the LORD is the beginning of wisdom, and knowledge of the Holy One is understanding" (Proverbs 9:10). While knowledge is valuable, God's wisdom transcends human logic. The greatest truths cannot be grasped by intellect alone, but must be revealed by the Spirit.

Gnosticism tried to reduce faith to abstract knowledge—just as rationalism and materialism do today. But the Bible affirms both reason and revelation, teaching that true faith requires trust in what lies *beyond* our full comprehension.

God does not call us to blind faith, but neither does He ask us to fully comprehend Him before we trust Him. Solomon said, "Trust in the LORD with all your heart and lean not on your own understanding" (Proverbs 3:5).

To worship God fully, we must reject the errors of both

ancient Gnosticism and modern rationalism. We need a faith that engages both head and heart, that seeks both truth and Spirit, that honors both reason and revelation.

This tension between reason and revelation is not just an abstract theological debate, it is shaping the direction of entire movements today. Around the world, we are witnessing a widening gap between those who embrace a supernatural, Spirit-empowered faith and those who reinterpret truth to fit cultural ideology.

THE CLASH OF TWO MOVEMENTS

In today's world, two of the largest and fastest-growing movements are heading toward an unavoidable collision:

- Pentecostal Christianity—the largest social movement in the Global South (Majority World), which emphasizes supernatural faith, spiritual gifts, and biblical authority.
- The LGBTQ Movement—one of the dominant social forces in the Western world, advocating for progressive sexual ethics, identity redefinition, and ideological influence in public life and the church.

Pentecostal and charismatic Christianity is now the fastest-growing expression of faith worldwide. By 2050, Pentecostals and charismatics are expected to number over one billion globally.[11]

Why is it growing? Because it proclaims a God who is not distant or theoretical, but powerfully present and actively at work in the world. Unlike much of Western rationalist Christianity, Pentecostal faith expects God to move—personally, powerfully, and supernaturally. In the Global South, Pentecostals reject philosophical materialism, scientism, and progressive sexual ethics. The movement thrives under persecution. In fact, whenever Christianity is suppressed, these churches tend to grow stronger, not weaker. It is a faith of action and encounter, not just intellectual belief.

By contrast, the LGBTQ movement has become one of the most influential ideological forces in Western nations. It has transformed culture, media, education, and even parts of the church. Legislation, corporate policy, and social pressure now enforce affirmation of LGBTQ ideology, with dissent often labeled as bigotry or hate speech.

Western mainline churches that have embraced LGBTQ theology are declining rapidly, while churches that uphold biblical sexuality—especially in the Global South—are growing rapidly.[12]

The LGBTQ movement, rooted in secularism and progressive ideology, is now embedded in Western political and cultural institutions. It appeals to the language of justice and inclusion, rightly echoing the moral language of the Civil Rights Movement. But it misapplies that framework to justify an unbiblical redefinition of identity and truth. Activists have framed their movement as a fight against oppression, which now demands ideological conformity. In many settings, failure to affirm LGBTQ identity can cost you your job, your reputation, or your place in society.

These two global movements offer fundamentally different versions of truth, morality, and human identity. One is built on the authority of Scripture and the expectation of God's supernatural power. The other is built on expressive individualism and cultural relativism. At this point, they cannot be reconciled. I have seen the clash of these two movements play out over and over in my years of pastoring. We've watched as many educated, progressive white Americans leave our church—and yet God continues to grow our community with Nigerians, Koreans, Brazilians, and others from the Global South.

And let me be clear: This is not about rejecting people. It's about rejecting lies that distort what God has made good. You can love someone and still disagree with the ideology shaping their worldview.

At some point, every believer must ask: Which will I follow—biblical faith or cultural ideology? The growing, global, Spirit-filled church, or the secularized Western movement that demands cultural and ideological conformity?

Now, to be clear: Some Christians may dismiss Pentecostalism over real concerns such as the prosperity gospel that distorts the gospel by focusing on health and wealth. Those critiques are valid. No movement is without its flaws, or beyond correction. Every movement needs a level of reformation. But the answer to bad theology is not skepticism—it's biblical truth.

We need the Pentecostal movement to counter our lukewarm and increasingly secular faith in the West. We need to recover supernatural expectation, evangelistic urgency, spiritual hunger, and biblical authority. We need churches that expect God to move, not just preach theology. We need to break free from rationalist skepticism and rediscover a faith that believes in miracles and transformation.

Before we critique Pentecostalism, we must be careful not to focus on the speck in our brother's eye while ignoring the plank in our own.[13] We should rightly reject distortions of the gospel—but we should not reject the movement God is using to bring revival across the world.

The question is, will we humble ourselves enough to receive it?

BEYOND REASON: ANOTHER MIRACLE THAT CHANGED MY LIFE

When I was in college, my aunt Kathy was diagnosed with a deadly form of pancreatic cancer. For the first time in my life, I felt led not just to pray, but to *fast and pray.* I didn't eat for three days, intentionally setting aside that time to intercede for her healing.

When she went in for surgery, the doctors were stunned. The cancer was gone. There was no trace. The doctors were dumbfounded. But my friends and family who prayed weren't. We knew it was God.

That was more than twenty-five years ago—and my aunt is still alive today, still testifying to the healing power of God.

Like the story from Kuwait, this was a reminder: Prayer moves heaven, miracles still happen, and our God is not limited by human logic. A faith stripped of the supernatural is not the faith Jesus gave us.

THE TRUTH: THERE IS A SUPERNATURAL DIMENSION

Jesus entrusted us with a mission far too big to accomplish without Him. He commanded us to make disciples of all nations and to go to the ends of the earth (Matthew 28:19–20).

In the Upper Room before His death, He made a profound promise: "Whoever believes in me will do the works I have been doing, and they will do even greater things than these" (John 14:12).

Christianity is supernatural at its core.

The very foundation of our faith rests on the miraculous—most significantly, the resurrection. Paul made this clear: "If Christ has not been raised, our preaching is useless and so is your faith" (1 Corinthians 15:14).

To believe in the miraculous is to believe that God does things that are beyond science or human explanation. It could be protection in a dangerous situation, a precise answer to prayer, unexpected financial provision, physical healing, or a broken relationship restored.

These things cannot always be rationally explained, but they are undeniably real. Every Christian has a testimony of God's supernatural work. At minimum, every Christian believes in the miraculous bodily resurrection of Jesus.

Paul understood this need for supernatural, not just rational, encounters with God when he wrote: "My message and my preaching were not with wise and persuasive words, but with a demonstration of the Spirit's power" (1 Corinthians 2:4–5).

Jesus understood it too: "A time is coming and has now come when the true worshipers will worship the Father in the *Spirit* and in truth" (John 4:23).

To believe in the miraculous is to believe that God does things that are beyond science or human explanation.

True worship must engage the head and the heart. They must move in the same direction. In other words, faith is *beyond* reason but is not *against* reason. "By faith we understand that the universe was formed at God's command, so that what is seen was not made out of what was visible" (Hebrews 11:3).

The witness of God is this: He doesn't contradict reason—He transcends it.

Jesus embodies both divine mystery and rational truth in perfect harmony. He is fully God (Spirit) and fully man (incarnate). His resurrection, which is historically verified, defies human logic—and yet it stands at the very center of our faith.[14] It reminds us that God's reality is greater than human reason.

THE COMMITMENT: WALKING IN THE SPIRIT (SPIRIT-FILLED LIVING)

The invitation here is simple but profound: Live a Spirit-filled life in an age of increasing skepticism.

Skeptical believers often feel torn—inclined to resist the work of the Holy Spirit for fear of losing intellectual integrity. But Jesus shows us that it's not necessary to choose between the head and the heart. In His life and ministry, reason and revelation moved in harmony.

The Spirit-filled life is marked by a hunger to discover and operate in the gifts God has given. And these are not reserved for a select few. They are available to everyone who has surrendered their life to Christ.

God isn't looking for people who have it all together. He's looking for willing hearts—hearts He can supernaturally equip.

Spiritual gifts aren't discovered through passive observation. They're discovered through active service. They're given to build up the church and bless the world.

The Bible teaches about these gifts in several places:

- **1 Corinthians 12**—***Manifestation gifts:*** Prophecy, tongues, healing, words of knowledge, miracles, faith, discernment
- **Romans 12**—***Service gifts:*** Mercy, hospitality, administration, generosity, exhortation
- **Ephesians 4**—***Leadership gifts:*** Prophesying, serving, teaching, exhortation, generosity, leadership, mercy

A healthy, growing church operates in all these gifts.

A healthy, growing believer operates in at least one.

You don't get to choose your gift(s), but you do get to decide whether you'll exercise it.[15]

Paul encouraged us: "Follow the way of love and eagerly desire gifts of the Spirit" (1 Corinthians 14:1).

If you don't yet know your spiritual gift(s), ask God to reveal it. Study what Scripture says. Seek guidance from your church leaders and godly peers who can help you discern. The Spirit loves to give good gifts—and He delights to see you walk in them.

Even in the early church, Paul recognized the temptation to reject the supernatural. That's why he warned: "My brothers and sisters, be eager to prophesy, and do not forbid speaking in tongues" (1 Corinthians 14:39).

After His resurrection, Jesus knew His disciples couldn't fulfill the Great Commission in their own strength. So, He breathed on them and said, "Receive the Holy Spirit" (John 20:22).

This was a preview of what was to come. At Pentecost, the outpouring of the Spirit began the fulfillment of Joel's prophecy: "In the last days, God says, I will pour out my Spirit on all people" (Acts 2:17; Joel 2:28). That outpouring continues today—until Christ returns.

Jesus promised: "You will receive power when the Holy Spirit comes on you; and you will be my witnesses in Jerusalem, and in all Judea and Samaria, and to the ends of the earth" (Acts 1:8).

This lie—that everything must be rational—forces us all to wrestle with foundational questions of discipleship:

- What do I believe about the Holy Spirit?
- Has the Holy Spirit been just a distant concept—or the One who awakens my heart to Christ each day?

- Have I eagerly desired to discover and use the gifts He has given me?
- Do I believe God still works miracles?

These are not abstract questions. They shape the kind of life we live and the kind of church we become. To reject the Spirit's work is to settle for a faith that lacks power. But to surrender—to truly yield to the Spirit—is to step into the life Jesus intended: a life full of wonder, full of purpose, and full of supernatural strength.

SURRENDER TO GOD'S SPIRIT

The key to experiencing this supernatural dimension of faith and spiritual gifting lies in one thing: our willingness to fully surrender to God's Spirit.

Jesus promised to build His church on a specific confession—Peter's declaration: "You are the Messiah, the Son of the Living God" (Matthew 16:16).

Some churches may have strong community. They may do good work in the world. But if they are not built on this foundational truth, they lack the power Jesus promised. They are not founded on the conviction that Jesus is the only way, the only truth, and the only life. And it is precisely within that confession that real power is found.

When we declare Jesus as Lord, we gain access to the supernatural power of the Holy Spirit:

- the power to bind and loose
- the power to heal the sick
- the power to pray for transformation
- the power to stand against spiritual darkness with courage and authority

The church was never meant to be a social club or simply a nonprofit organization. It was meant to be a Spirit-empowered people, actively engaged in the mission of God. Jesus assured us of this promise and power: "I will build my church, and the gates of hell shall not prevail against it" (Matthew 16:18, ESV).

A CALL TO FAITH-FILLED OBEDIENCE

The local church is the most exciting and transformative community in the world. It's the one place where everyone has a role—where God gives spiritual gifts and supernatural power to all who confess Christ.

Not just to pastors or leaders. Not just to those who seem "spiritually advanced."

But to every believer. Including you.

God's plan to change the world has always included His people. His mission didn't end with the resurrection—it continues through you. He chooses to work through imperfect people to accomplish His perfect plan.

This has always been the case.

Moses was tending sheep when God called to him from a burning bush. *Go to Pharaoh and tell him to let My people go.* But Moses, like many of us, pushed back: "Who am I that I should go to Pharaoh?" he protested. "I am slow of speech and tongue" (Exodus 3:11; 4:10).

Jeremiah had his excuses too: "I do not know how to speak; I am too young" (Jeremiah 1:6).

Peter, after denying Jesus three times, believed he had disqualified himself for good.

And yet, God didn't listen to their excuses. He called them anyway. And He equipped them as they obeyed.

That's how the Spirit works. He doesn't call the ones who already feel ready. He calls those who feel weak, unqualified, and afraid.

Maybe you've felt the same way. Maybe you've sensed God nudging you toward something, but doubt has whispered all the reasons you shouldn't step out in faith.

- I'm too young.
- I'm too old.
- I don't have the education.
- I don't have the resources.
- I don't know the right people.
- I've made too many mistakes.
- God wouldn't use someone like me.

But the Bible tells a different story: "God chose the foolish things of the world to shame the wise; God chose the weak things of the world to shame the strong" (1 Corinthians 1:27).

If we could accomplish God's plan in our own strength, we would take the credit. But when He uses the weak, the unlikely, and the overlooked, there's no mistaking who gets the glory.

And I know this is true—because He's done it in my life.

THE INVITATION: A SUPERNATURAL LIFE

The invitation is clear: Step out in faith. Desire the gifts. Embrace the supernatural life of the Spirit. Worship in Spirit and in truth. "Do not quench the Spirit. Do not treat prophecies with contempt but test them all; hold on to what is good" (1 Thessalonians 5:19–21).

We are not called to live safe, calculated, comfortable lives.

We are called to live boldly—trusting in the power of the Holy Spirit, and stepping into places that only God can sustain.

That's what it means to resist rational skepticism and walk in Spirit-filled power.

As A. W. Tozer once said, "God is looking for people through whom He can do the impossible. What a pity that we plan only the things we can do ourselves."[16]

This is your moment of decision.

Will you let fear hold you back?

Or will you step forward in faith—even when you don't feel ready, even when the plan doesn't make sense?

As we move further into an age dominated by skepticism and rationalism, it's not just miracles and the supernatural that are rejected—it's also the grace of God in how we treat one another.

A worldview built on rationalism often leaves little room for humility, forgiveness, or love. The same forces that train us to filter faith through skepticism also train us to dismiss, cancel, and cut off those who disagree with us.

And that is the final lie we must confront.

DISCUSSION AND REFLECTION QUESTIONS

Lie 6: Everything Is Rational

1. **Head vs. Heart**

   Have you ever felt tension between your head and your heart? In what ways has reason strengthened your faith, and in what ways has it challenged it?

2. **The Limits of Rationalism**

   Rationalism says that only what is logical and explainable is true. What are the dangers of elevating human reason above divine revelation?

3. **Faith Beyond Understanding**

   Paul wrote that God's wisdom often appears foolish to the world (1 Corinthians 1:25). How does this challenge the modern assumption that faith must be fully explainable?

4. **The Role of Mystery in Faith**

   Jesus often spoke in parables and performed miracles that defied logic. Why do you think God allows mystery to be a part of faith? How can you learn to embrace the unknown rather than fear it?

5. **Scientism vs. Faith**

   How does scientism (the belief that only science provides truth) influence how people view faith today? How can Christians affirm the value of science while still believing in the supernatural?

6. **Materialism and the Unseen World**

   Paul said, "We fix our eyes not on what is seen, but on what is unseen" (2 Corinthians 4:18). In what ways does materialism blind people to spiritual realities? How can you counteract this mindset?

7. **Doubt vs. Skepticism**

   What is the difference between healthy doubt that leads to deeper faith and skepticism that erodes belief? How can you make space for questions without allowing them to define your faith?

8. **The Skeptical Believer**

   Looking back, have you ever taken on the identity of a skeptical believer? How can someone move from being controlled by skepticism to embracing faith with trust?

9. **Experiencing the Supernatural**

   The Bible describes a God of power who performs miracles and moves supernaturally. Have you experienced God's power in your life? If not, what might be keeping you from seeking or recognizing it?

10. **Walking in the Spirit**

    Paul commanded believers to "eagerly desire gifts of the Spirit" (1 Corinthians 14:1). What practical steps can you take to live a Spirit-filled life, rather than one that is purely intellectual?

7

WHEN CONFLICT DIVIDES

From Cancel Culture to Radical Forgiveness

> There is one good point which both these churches have in common—they are both party churches. I think I warned you before that if your patient can't be kept out of the Church, he ought at least to be violently attached to some party within it. I don't mean on really doctrinal issues; about those, the more lukewarm he is the better.
>
> —*The Screwtape Letters,* Letter 16

During his time as vice president, Mike Pence occasionally attended our church. We're located just north of the White House, right in the heart of Washington, D.C., a prime spot for political leaders who spend their weekends in the city.

But here's the thing: D.C. is overwhelmingly liberal. Over 90 percent of voters in our city supported the Democratic candidate in the last five presidential elections.[1] So as you might imagine, the vice president's presence stirred some tension among folks in our church who didn't share his political views.

Some were ready to leave the church. And it wasn't just the added inconvenience of Secret Service screening; it was the weight of the policies his administration represented.

One church member emailed me in frustration, "I do not adhere to the politics of the current administration."

I heard versions of this concern repeatedly as I tried to pastor people through that season. But then this same member wrote something unexpected:

> I ended up sitting right behind VP Pence on the first Sunday of his visit in May, and in the same row with him a couple weeks later. Even in D.C., you can imagine my surprise to see such a public figure in church. On that second service, we took communion, and it ended up being a moment of deep conviction for me. Here I was, taking the bread and cup with a brother in Christ. God reminded me that in God's eyes, the vice president and I are the same: flawed, beloved, children. Despite my beliefs about Mike Pence's politics, I realized I am no better than he in the eyes of the Lord.

She closed by saying, "I can imagine it's been a challenge to manage the politics and logistics of having the vice president at services, but do know that at least in my case, God has been using his presence here."

This lie is about unforgiveness.

One of the greatest challenges we face as Christians today is this: How do we maintain relationship amid difference? How do we love our brothers and sisters in Christ when their political convictions clash with our own?

If we don't learn to do this, the church will devolve into an echo chamber—filled with people who look, vote, and think just like we do.

But that is not the historic witness of the church. And it

certainly is not the way of Jesus. Jesus came to cross boundaries—and to call people from every tribe, tongue, and nation into His kingdom.

THE LIE: ENEMIES MUST BE CANCELED

The lie that many Christians believe is that *enemies must be canceled*. That anyone who disagrees with us should be cut off, unfriended, or exiled from our life.

It's a deeply secular lie, born not of Scripture but of a culture that thrives on division. And it manifests on both the Right and the Left.

On the Right, it looks like branding fellow believers as "woke" for talking about injustice. Pastors get labeled Marxists for preaching on systemic sin and its harms. Advocating for refugees or wearing a mask during COVID was enough to split entire churches.

On the Left, believers who hold a traditional sexual ethic—even with compassion—are called bigots. Professors are pressured to resign. Friends get ghosted for voting differently. Churches that don't display a Black Lives Matter sign and hang a rainbow flag out front are seen as unsafe.

In both cases, faith becomes secondary to tribal allegiance. Instead of bearing with one another in love, we bail. Instead of correcting gently, we cancel.

This lie convinces us that to love someone means compromising our convictions. That we have to give up our values to stay in relationship.

Jesus never compromised truth—but He also never abandoned love. The enemy loves this lie because it divides. Jesus warned us, "The thief comes only to steal and kill and destroy" (John 10:10). When we buy into cancel culture, we give the enemy permission to do all three—stealing our unity, killing our witness, and destroying the very relationships that God will use to sanctify us.

The church is increasingly importing the secular strategies of the world. Leaders build platforms by stoking outrage. Churchgoers choose congregations based not on spiritual formation or biblical truth, but on whether a pastor affirms their pre-existing political views.

Instead of submitting to Christ as Lord, we treat Him as a garnish sprinkled on top of whatever political ideology we already hold.

When we buy into cancel culture, we give the enemy permission to do all three—stealing our unity, killing our witness, and destroying the very relationships that God will use to sanctify us.

The secular playbook Christians are adopting on both sides mirrors Saul Alinsky's *Rules for Radicals,* which teaches that we must polarize to mobilize.

In his thirteenth rule, Alinsky advises organizers to "Pick the target, freeze it, personalize it, and polarize it."[2] In other words: isolate your opponent, demonize them, and draw a clear line between "us" and "them."

He writes: "Before men can act an issue must be polarized. Men will act when they are convinced that their cause is 100 percent on the side of the angels and that the opposition are 100 percent on the side of the devil."[3]

The tactic now fuels movements on both sides of the aisle—and many churches are following suit.

And the devil loves it. He would love for you to think your

brother or sister in Christ is the enemy—so you never get around to resisting the actual one.

Paul understood this temptation when he wrote to the Ephesian church: "Our struggle is not against flesh and blood, but against the rulers, against the authorities, against the powers of this dark world and against the spiritual forces of evil in the heavenly realms" (Ephesians 6:12).

The struggle is a spiritual one that manifests in the natural realm with actual people. But people are not your enemy. The devil is your enemy.

Once the enemy has you focused on another person or party, and preferably a fellow brother or sister in Christ, the next trick is to take a good value and make it an ultimate one. Take patriotism, for example. Screwtape tells Wormwood, "Let him begin by treating the Patriotism or the Pacifism as part of his religion. Then let him, under the influence of partisan spirit, come to regard it as the most important part."[4]

Patriotism is a noble value—loving your country, appreciating its strengths, and serving it with pride. There is nothing wrong with that. Too often, we focus on what we lack rather than the freedoms and opportunities we have. It's easy to take our liberties for granted. However, the enemy seeks to twist this devotion, turning it into an ultimate allegiance—one that elevates national identity above our faith. When our love for country overshadows our commitment to Christ, we risk making our faith subservient to national loyalty rather than keeping God at the center of our lives.

The same thing can happen with pacifism. Pursuing peace and rejecting violence is a deeply Christian ideal. But when peace becomes your central focus—when it causes you to avoid confrontation with evil or injustice—it can become a distorted form of self-righteousness. Instead of seeking reconciliation, you settle for passivity where confronting sin or injustice is ignored. Instead of loving your enemy, you avoid them.

This is the enemy's strategy:

1. Turn your brother into your enemy.
2. Elevate a secondary value above your ultimate allegiance to Christ.
3. Cancel the person entirely.

And this last step—canceling a brother or sister in Christ—is something our culture seems to have perfected.

CANCEL CULTURE

When it was announced that Passion leader Louie Giglio would give the benediction at President Obama's second inauguration, advisers erupted over a sermon he'd preached in the 1990s that briefly mentioned homosexuality. Within days, he stepped down from the role amid intense pressure—despite years of humanitarian work and no recent controversial statements.[5] That swift disinvitation illustrates cancel culture in action: one past comment, no room for context, no chance for dialogue.

This example is mild in comparison to others. What may have started as a call to accountability can quickly morph into a culture of public shaming—where reputations are destroyed, jobs are lost, and social standing is erased, often without any real discussion or due process. Cancel culture thrives on social media, where a single comment, an old post, or an unpopular stance can trigger an avalanche of outrage.

At its worst, cancel culture leaves no room for grace. It demands swift and severe punishment without considering intent, personal growth, or the possibility of change. Instead of inviting honest dialogue, it shuts it down—making people more afraid of being canceled than of engaging meaningfully with difficult issues.

At its best, cancel culture is really just accountability. There's nothing wrong with expecting public figures, pastors, or even everyday people to take responsibility when they say or do something harmful or sinful. When done right, it can shine a light on injustice, push for meaningful change, and hold those in power to a higher standard.

In fact, some voices wouldn't have been heard without the pressure of public outcry. And there are times when calling someone out is justified—like when someone refuses to acknowledge wrongdoing or continues in abusive behavior without consequence. In those cases, accountability isn't just appropriate; it's biblical. We are called to speak the truth and stand up for what's right.

But here is the deeper question: Are we seeking restoration or just tearing someone down? The Pharisees were the original cancel culture enforcers. They were quick to call people out, publicly shame them, and push people to the margins of society for failing to meet their standards. They weaponized religious law to cut off those they deemed unclean—not just from the synagogue, but from community, and often from any hope of redemption.

We see this play out again and again in the Gospels. The Pharisees were constantly looking to discredit Jesus, trying to "cancel" Him in front of the crowds. They called Him a blasphemer, accused Him of breaking the Sabbath, and ultimately sought to silence Him by plotting His death. When Jesus healed on the Sabbath or dined with sinners, they didn't rejoice in the lives being changed—they were outraged that their rules had been broken.

One of the clearest examples is in John 8, with the woman caught in adultery. The Pharisees dragged her before Jesus, ready to stone her—not to seek justice, but to trap Jesus in a spectacle.

But Jesus flipped the script: "Let any one of you who is without sin be the first to throw a stone at her" (verse 7). In that moment, He exposed the heart of cancel culture—a heart quick to condemn but slow to show mercy.

THE COUNTERFEIT IDENTITY: THE DIVISIVE INFLUENCER

Believing the lie that enemies must be canceled leads to the formation of a false identity: the Divisive Influencer.

It starts with the justification of influence—people are listening, clicks are happening, the metrics are up. But underneath it all, something more dangerous is happening.

The real danger isn't just the divisive behavior. The deeper danger is allowing your very identity to be shaped in opposition to others, rather than by something greater than yourself. You become known more for what you're against than for what you are for. Consider journalist Julie Roys. While at times her investigations have exposed real abuse and corruption in the church, her platform has become more associated with takedowns than with a redemptive vision for the body of Christ.

A Divisive Influencer is someone who thrives on conflict. They stir up division and create an "us versus them" mentality. They are more concerned with winning arguments than seeking truth, more focused on tearing people down than building them up. Their influence doesn't unify—it polarizes. Rather than calling people toward grace, they amplify outrage, encourage hostility, and use controversy to elevate themselves at the expense of others.

In cancel culture, these voices are often the loudest voices in the room. They are the ones leading the charge, feeding the frenzy, and ensuring that whoever is in the spotlight of condemnation is cast out with no path to redemption.

We've seen this before. The Pharisees thrived on public shaming and condemnation. If someone didn't meet their standard—whether it was a tax collector, a "sinner," or even Jesus—they didn't just challenge them; they tried to erase their credibility and remove them from influence entirely.

But Jesus showed a radically different way. He didn't ignore sin, but He also didn't weaponize it. He confronted wrongdoing, yes—but always while offering a way forward. Where the Pharisees saw people as disposable, Jesus saw them as redeemable.

Cancel culture—and the Divisive Influencers who drive it—leave no room for grace. But the way of Jesus is truth and love. His goal is always restoration, not destruction.

COUNTERFEIT JUSTICE

In 2015, Kelvin J. Cochran—the African American fire chief of Atlanta—was suspended and then forced to resign after distributing a book he authored among his department that expressed biblical views on adultery and homosexuality. He wasn't charged with misconduct—only punished for holding and expressing biblical beliefs.[6] While Alliance Defending Freedom later successfully represented him in a religious freedom lawsuit, the swift termination without conversation, investigation, or path to reconciliation perfectly illustrates how public institutions can enact moral censure without grace.

Cancel culture is a product of secular belief. It thrives in a world that has rejected God's authority and replaced it with a shifting, self-made morality. In today's culture, personal experience defines truth, and the greatest sin is to offend the dominant cultural narrative. There is no grace, no redemption—only a relentless pursuit of ideological purity, where one wrong step can cost you everything.

Cancel culture leaves no room for God. It strips away divine authority and replaces it with the ever-shifting standards of public opinion, where human outrage becomes the final judge.

At its core, cancel culture is a secular imitation of justice—not the kind of justice pursued through courts or due process, but a social form of moral reckoning that mimics biblical accountability while eliminating grace. It demands confession without forgiveness. It imposes consequences but offers no restoration. There is no space for transformation—only exile. The mob becomes judge, jury, and executioner.

We see this same pattern in some expressions of progressive Christianity, a theology shaped more by culture than by the authority of Scripture. Many churches embrace secular activism disguised as justice, unaware of how it contradicts the gospel. They borrow the language of righteousness but remove the cross. They call for activism but leave no room for repentance or grace. Cancel culture offers a counterfeit gospel—one obsessed with punishment but incapable of redemption.

THE TRAP OF DIVISIVE ZEAL

Most Divisive Influencers don't rise to prominence on their own. We help make them. It starts subtly: a bold post, a fiery quote, a viral clip that "says what we're all thinking." We click, like, share, repost. We applaud their courage. And little by little, we confuse outrage with faithfulness. The more divisive they become, the more attention they get—not in spite of their anger, but because of it.

At first, they seem like prophets—voices crying out against compromise. But over time, their platforms become echo chambers of rage. And we're still there—amening in the comments, defending their harshest words, dismissing critics as soft or worldly. We convince ourselves they're just telling it like it is. But what we're really doing is feeding the algorithm of division.

Some of us stop listening to our own pastor because a louder voice online seems more "biblical." Some of us disengage from our local church because the influencer we follow makes every church look suspect. In our desire for bold truth, we don't realize we've been discipled by someone who's more interested in exposing sin than redeeming sinners.

Most Divisive Influencers don't rise to prominence on their own. We help make them.

This is the trap of divisive zeal: not just that someone gets radicalized, but that we reward them for it. We might think we're standing for truth, but if there's no grace, we're just adding noise. Jesus spoke hard truths—but always with the goal of healing, not humiliating.

The road back begins with humility—not just for the influencer, but for us. A church that stops rewarding outrage can start rebuilding trust. A people rooted in love can still tell the truth, but they'll do it in a way that sounds like Jesus.

Cancel culture stands in stark contrast to Jesus' command: *Love your enemies.*

THE TRUTH: LOVE YOUR ENEMIES

Jesus famously told His disciples in the Sermon on the Mount:

> You have heard that it was said, "Love your neighbor and hate your enemy." But I tell you, love your enemies and pray for those who persecute you, that you may be children of your Father in heaven. He causes his sun to rise on the evil and the good, and sends rain on the righteous and the unrighteous. If you love those who love you, what reward will you get? Are not even the tax collectors doing that? (Matthew 5:43–46)

Jesus' command to love our enemies was revolutionary. In Jewish culture, loving one's neighbor was already required by the Law (Leviticus 19:18), but hating one's enemy had become an unspoken norm—especially under Roman occupation. Religious leaders often reinforced an "us versus them" mentality, viewing Gentiles, tax collectors, and sinners not as people to be loved, but as enemies to be avoided.

Jesus flipped the script by commanding His followers not only to reject hatred but to actively love, bless, and pray for those who persecuted them. This wasn't just countercultural—it was shocking. The Pharisees and Zealots expected a Messiah who would destroy their enemies, not one who would call them to forgive and love them. In a world where power and revenge were seen as virtues, responding to persecution with love was unheard of.

This teaching remains one of the clearest distinctions between Jesus and every other moral teacher of His time. No other philosophy, religion, or political system in that era promoted unconditional love for one's enemies as the path to righteousness and identity as children of God (Matthew 5:45). Jesus was calling His followers to reflect the heart of the Father, who extends grace to both the righteous and the unrighteous.

And this isn't just hard—it is humanly impossible apart from the transforming power of God's love. That's why it remains one of the most radical and defining marks of a true disciple.

Honestly, loving my enemies is a topic I'd rather avoid. It feels unnatural. I'd prefer not to wrestle with these words from Jesus, because they force me to reflect deeply—and they challenge me at every level.

Yet it's precisely in this place of dependence on God that I've seen His power most at work in me.

When we step into what God is calling us to—especially when it's hard, when it brings conflict or even suffering—we begin to experience His transformative strength.

Our culture tells us the goal is to avoid pain, to eliminate discomfort at all costs. But Jesus reverses that narrative. He teaches us that the kingdom of God advances not through comfort but through endurance—when we face persecution, suffering, and hatred, and still meet it with love.

ENEMY LOVE: A CORE CHRISTIAN WITNESS

Enemy love is profoundly countercultural, yet it is precisely what enables us to maintain a distinctly Christian witness in an increasingly secular age.

Loving our enemies calls us to move beyond simply following the letter of the law and to embrace the deeper spirit of the law. We must learn to go further than the world's standards, which often say, "Don't hurt people. Don't cause any harm or say anything too nasty online." Jesus calls us to something far greater.

A powerful example is found in the life of Dr. King who knew that loving your enemies didn't mean being passive or compromising on justice. Rather, he saw enemy love as essential to pursuing true justice.

At Dr. King's homegoing service, Dr. Benjamin Mays, his mentor and longtime president of Morehouse College, said:

> This man was loved by some and hated by others. If any man knew the meaning of suffering, King knew. House bombed; living day by day for 13 years under constant threats of death; maliciously accused of being a Communist; falsely accused of being insincere and seeking limelight for his own glory; stabbed by a member of his own race; slugged in a hotel lobby; jailed 30 times; occasionally deeply hurt because his friends betrayed him—and yet this man had no bitterness in his heart, no rancor in his soul, no revenge in his mind; and he went up and down the length and breadth of this world preaching nonviolence and the redemptive power of love. He believed with all of his heart, mind and soul that the way to peace and brotherhood is through nonviolence, love and suffering.[7]

King wasn't the only voice for racial and economic justice in his day. What made him distinct was his countercultural methodology—the way of Jesus outlined in the Sermon on the Mount. And it bore lasting fruit.

King often said he didn't need to *like* someone to *love* them. He didn't need to agree with their words, actions, or beliefs. But he could still love them.[8]

Loving our enemies doesn't mean being a doormat—Dr. King certainly was not. It means being willing to suffer, as Jesus did, to help advance the kingdom of God. It means meeting hatred, violence, and injustice with love—because only then can the cycle of violence be broken.

Jesus' call is not to ignore evil—His mission is to overcome it. But He urges us to resist it without resorting to violence.

When we respond to hate with love, something shifts. We catch our enemies off guard. We disarm them in a way that goes beyond the physical. A spiritual disruption takes place that can reach the soul of a person.

Exercising grace in the face of evil exposes it more powerfully than retaliation ever could. Our response highlights the wrong without adding fuel to the fire.

Dr. King once told the story of driving at night in Tennessee. Other drivers weren't dimming their lights when they passed. King's brother got mad and said, "The next car that comes along here and refuses dim the lights, I'm gonna fail to dim mine."

King replied, "Oh no, don't do that. There'd be too much light on this highway, and it will end up in mutual destruction for all. Somebody has got to have some sense on this highway . . . to dim the lights."[9]

In Matthew 5:43–46, Jesus is essentially saying, "Dim the lights." He isn't calling us to disengage or stop fighting for justice. Rather, He's calling us to de-escalate in order to engage in the deeper soul work that political systems can't bring about. Lasting change requires inner transformation, and that only happens when we choose love over retaliation.

Nonviolence is not passive, nor is it about being weak. It's a powerful act that disrupts the principalities and powers that are behind the evil actions we face. As Scripture reminds us, we wrestle not against flesh and blood, but against the spiritual forces of evil.[10]

PRAYING FOR OUR ENEMIES

The first call of Jesus is to nonretaliation. But the second is active love.

As Augustine of Hippo said, "Many have learned how to offer the other cheek, but do not know how to love him by whom they were struck."[11]

Prayer will expose what is in your heart. You cannot genuinely pray for someone you hate.

Jesus commands us not only to resist revenge but to love our enemies by praying for them. This moves us from playing defense to playing offense—from doing the minimum required to seeking deeper transformation. As Alfred Plummer puts it:

> To return evil for good is devilish;
> to return good for good is human;
> to return good for evil is divine.
> To love as God loves is moral perfection,
> and this perfection Christ tells us to aim for.[12]

It's when you return good for evil that you begin to hunger for righteousness and thirst for the gospel to be tangible and evident to all.

The real test of whether you are playing offense is simple: Are you praying for your enemies? Prayer will expose what is in your heart. You cannot genuinely pray for someone you hate.

I've found it far easier to pray for distant enemies—figures like Vladimir Putin, Kim Jong-Un, or Xi Jinping—than for the political enemies closer to home.

Years ago, I was part of a group that met with Mahmoud Ahmadinejad during his presidency of Iran. Dozens of religious leaders gathered with one of the world's most polarizing and oppressive rulers. The spiritual warfare in the room was palpable. Yet I found it almost easy to pray for him. It made me feel like I was checking the box—doing my Christian duty.

But praying for political enemies in my own country? Especially family members who fiercely support them? That's much harder.

My question for you is this: Do you genuinely pray for the leader of the opposing political party? And I don't mean prayers like "God, save them from their wickedness." Do you pray for their salvation? For wisdom? For blessing?

I'll never forget visiting Gordon Cosby in his tiny apartment above Christ House, just down the street from our church. Gordon, the founder of Church of the Savior, helped start countless ministries across D.C.—Potter's House, Joseph's House, Samaritan Inns, Jubilee Housing, and many more.

I'll never forget one meeting I had with him when he was in his nineties. I asked him when we entered: "What have you been up to today?" He responded in a completely serious voice, "Praying for President Bush." This was during the Iraq War, a time when Gordon disagreed strongly with Bush's policies on the war. He continued, "The Holy Spirit told me I need to pray for him all day every day. It's so hard, but I've prayed for him ninety-five times today."

Gordon didn't pray because he agreed with Bush's policies. He prayed because he understood Jesus' call.

And I believe this may be one of the most urgent tasks before us in this generation: To love our political enemies. To see them first as human beings. To understand their stories, their hopes, and fears.

The church father Chrysostom, who ministered in the fourth century, called praying for enemies the "very highest summit of self-control."[13] He outlined nine ascending steps to enemy love with the highest being "Entreat God Himself on his behalf" through *prayer*.[14]

He placed intercessory prayer at the pinnacle of maturity of these nine steps.

Why pray for our enemies? Jesus answered clearly: "That you may be children of your Father in heaven. He causes his sun to rise on the evil and the good, and sends rain on the righteous and the unrighteous" (Matthew 5:45).

God extends two types of grace. There is *saving grace,* which is God's supernatural work that brings sinners to repentance and salvation.[15] And there is *common grace,* which God gives to all humanity: the beauty of creation, talents and abilities, a conscience to discern right from wrong.

It is this common grace Jesus refers to in Matthew 5:45, which we are called to reflect to our enemies: loving them, even when they do not share our values or beliefs.

God does not want us to discriminate in our love and prayers. This does not mean abandoning truth, but it does mean seeing people as God sees them.

There are some things we need to leave to God's

judgment—some injustices that can only be righted in His timing. And when we do, we are freed. Freed from the obsession of defending ourselves. Freed from the need to settle every score.

MAINTAIN RELATIONSHIP AMONG DIFFERENCE

In today's polarized world, one of the greatest tests of Christian humility is maintaining relationship despite deep differences. Families, churches, and communities are being torn apart over politics, ideology, and identity. The temptation is to withdraw from those who don't see the world the way we do. But Jesus calls us to a different path—one marked by grace, humility, and connection. He didn't say, "Blessed are those who win arguments," but, "Blessed are the peacemakers" (Matthew 5:9). To follow Him means choosing people over polarization.

The early church modeled this kind of unity. Jews and Gentiles, rich and poor, politically opposed groups came together not because they agreed on everything, but because they were united in Christ. Their witness wasn't uniformity, it was love across difference. Peacemaking doesn't mean avoiding hard conversations or pretending disagreements don't matter. It means engaging them with humility, refusing to weaponize our convictions, and prayerfully working for relationships to endure.

Our ability to stay connected, especially when it's hard, is one of the most powerful testimonies we can offer. As Jesus prayed in John 17, our unity is how the world will know we belong to Him. The way we navigate disagreement—especially in the church—reveals whether our faith is truly shaped by the cross. When we love across divides, we show the world a better way.

THE COMMITMENT: FORGIVING THOSE WHO HURT YOU (RADICAL FORGIVENESS)

There is no peacemaking or reconciliation without forgiveness.

Jesus taught us in the Lord's Prayer to say, "Forgive us our sins, as we forgive those who sin against us" (Luke 11:4, NLT). He added a sobering warning at the end, saying, "If you forgive other people when they sin against you, your heavenly Father will also forgive you. But if you do not forgive others their sins, your Father will not forgive your sins" (Matthew 6:14–15).

It is easy to make forgiveness something we do in our hearts and minds but that is divorced from our actions.

One of the most powerful examples of this comes from Dieudonné Nahimana, a Burundian pastor and presidential candidate whose life is a profound testament to forgiveness and reconciliation.

During Burundi's civil war, Dieudonné's father was tragically murdered. As a teenager living on the streets of Bujumbura, he experienced a radical conversion to Christ. Instead of seeking retaliation against those who killed his father, he chose the path of forgiveness. And for Dieudonné, it went beyond words: He forgave the man responsible, and even took the remarkable step of sponsoring the education of that man's children for decades.

This act of forgiveness was not isolated. It became the foundation of Dieudonné's broader commitment to healing and peace in Burundi. He went on to found New Generation, an organization dedicated to supporting street children and promoting reconciliation. Through New Generation, he has trained thousands of young people in peacebuilding, bringing together former perpetrators and victims to work side by side for a better future.

I had the opportunity to see Dieudonné's work firsthand in Burundi, and to meet the family he supports, the very family whose father killed his own. His testimony challenges me to reconsider what true forgiveness looks like, especially when so many of the situations I face seem elementary compared to what he has endured.[16]

Forgiveness is not weakness. It is the courageous, costly path that leads to freedom—and the clearest evidence of the gospel at work in us.

THE POWER TO LOVE OUR ENEMIES

Forgiveness does not come naturally to us. It requires repentance—not just on the surface, but deep in the heart.

When Jesus calls us to love our enemies, He is not asking us to do something humanly achievable. He is inviting us to something supernatural, something only possible through the power of the gospel.

The reality is, we can't love our enemies on our own. God's standards are too high for fallen humanity. The spirit may be willing, but the flesh is weak. How can we ever be poor in spirit, meek, and pure in heart? How can we pray sincerely for those who have wronged us?

We can't—at least not by human effort.

And that realization is a gift.

Because it drives us back to the cross.

It forces us to admit that we need a new heart. We need new life.

The apostle Paul said it this way: "I have been crucified with Christ and I no longer live, but Christ lives in me. The life I now live in the body, I live by faith in the Son of God, who loved me and gave himself for me" (Galatians 2:20).

Through Christ, and by the indwelling power of the Holy Spirit, we are given the ability to live differently. To hunger and thirst for righteousness. To love when hated. To forgive when wronged. To pray with new authority and see healing where there was once only hurt.

This is the miracle of the Christian life: What we cannot do in our own strength, God accomplishes through His Spirit in us.

Do you know Christ personally?

Have you experienced the power of His resurrection?

Have you been crucified with Him and raised to a new way of living?

Because only when Christ lives in us can we love as He loves—especially when it comes to loving our enemies.

And when we do, we reveal not only the depth of our own transformation. We reveal the very heart of God to a watching world.

DISCUSSION AND REFLECTION QUESTIONS

Lie 7: Enemies Must Be Canceled

1. **The Temptation to Cancel**

   How have you personally encountered the temptation to cancel others—whether in your church, in your family, or online? What is the danger of adopting this cancel culture mindset?
2. **The Divide Between Political Ideologies**

   How does our current political climate contribute to the division you see in the church? Have you noticed any examples of "us versus them" mentalities in your own church or community?
3. **The Challenge of Loving Enemies**

   What does Jesus' command to "love your enemies" mean to you? How do you reconcile this teaching with your natural reactions toward those who oppose you politically or personally?
4. **Pacifism vs. Biblical Peace**

   In what ways does pacifism, though noble, become distorted into an idol? How can you embrace the peace that Christ offers while still standing for justice and confronting evil?
5. **The Pharisees as Divisive Influencers**

   In what ways did the Pharisees act as Divisive Influencers in the Gospels? How can you avoid falling into a similar role of condemnation and cancellation in your own life?
6. **The Root of Divisive Influencers**

   Why do you think some Christians become Divisive Influencers? How does the enemy twist good intentions, like a desire for truth, into something that causes division?

7. **The Role of Accountability**

   How do you distinguish between the biblical call to accountability and the destructive nature of cancel culture? What does true accountability look like in the context of Christian community?

8. **Recognizing the True Enemy**

   How can you shift your perspective from seeing other people as the enemy to understanding that our true enemy is the spiritual forces of evil? What practical steps can you take to fight spiritual battles rather than getting caught in flesh-and-blood conflicts?

9. **Peacemaking and Political Differences**

   What does it look like to be a peacemaker in today's polarized world? How can you actively love and engage with those who hold political views opposite to your own, especially within the church?

10. **A Personal Next Step**

    What is one concrete step you can take this week to begin practicing enemy love in your own relationships—whether it's with someone in your family, workplace, or political sphere? How can you shift from reacting with anger or frustration to responding with love and grace?

8

JUST IMAGINE

A Revival Generation

> The great thing is to prevent his doing anything. As long as he does not convert it into action, it does not matter how much he thinks about this new repentance.
>
> —*The Screwtape Letters,* Letter 13

This is the book I should have written many years ago. I should have been more clear—first to my own church—that believing these lies doesn't just weaken our faith; it can ruin it.

These lies aren't just personally damaging, they are collectively destructive. They erode the soil where spiritual hunger grows. They numb our hearts. They quiet conviction. They suppress the Spirit's work. And unless they are resisted, they will keep us from the very outpouring of God's Spirit we desperately need.

We've walked together through seven of the most deceptive lies facing Christians today—lies that sound true, feel right, and often go unchallenged, even in the church. Lies that chip away at our resilience and invite us to drift:

- The self-centered worship that says faith is all about me.
- The spiritual isolation that says church is optional.
- The privatized faith that leads to lukewarm living.

- The selective faith that says the Bible is outdated.
- The performative activism that says charity is enough.
- The cold rationalism that leads to a skeptical spirit.
- The cancel culture mindset that believes influence comes through division.

The danger is these lies don't just weaken individual believers—they suffocate spiritual hunger and revival. They block the conviction of sin, deaden our sensitivity to God's presence, and dampen the visible evidence of true transformation.

But in response to these lies, we have recovered timeless biblical practices that help us stand firm with an unshakable faith:

- **True Worship** that invites us into a God-centered faith.
- **Deep Community** that invites us to be spiritually formed through the local church.
- **Bold Storytelling** that invites us to share our story with courage and authenticity.
- **Bible Engagement** that invites us to receive all of God's Word.
- **Biblical Justice** that invites us to pursue people with sacrificial love.
- **Spirit-Filled Living** that invites us to embrace both mystery and power.
- **Radical Forgiveness** that invites us to practice peacemaking in a divided world.

These are not just private disciplines. They are public declarations. They are how we prepare for revival in a culture desperate for hope.

Revival isn't just a moment we study in history—it's an invitation for us today.

And it begins with people who resist the lies and long for the truth.

The good news is you don't have to drift. You don't have to watch friends deconstruct and lose heart. You can resist the lies of the enemy and stand firm in a faith that is visible, resilient, and alive.

You can become a bearer of revival.

REVIVAL DEFINED: AWAKENING TO THE PRESENCE OF GOD

Revival is one of those words that Christians often throw around, but in Scripture and in history, it is anything but casual. Revival is a holy interruption. It is a sovereign move of God. It is a downpour of grace that no program or event can produce.

Dr. Martyn Lloyd-Jones described revival as "a period of unusual blessing and activity in the life of the Christian Church."[1]

James Burns says revival is when "large numbers of persons who have been dead or indifferent to spiritual realities then become intensely awakened to them."[2]

What is dead comes back to life. What is numb is stirred awake. What is routine becomes charged with urgency and fire.

God doesn't send revival into thin air. He sends it into prepared hearts.

Revival is not simply emotionalism or excitement. It is a move of God where hearts are broken over sin, captivated by grace, and emboldened by the Spirit to live in a way that is visible to the world.

In their book on this topic, James Choung and Ryan Pfeiffer state that every true revival brings breakthrough in three areas:[3]

- **Word**—The Word of God comes alive. We crave Scripture and faithful preaching.
- **Deed**—The gospel becomes tangible. We live out sacrificial acts of justice and mercy.
- **Power**—The Spirit shows up. We witness miracles, experience freedom, and stand in awe as countless lives are transformed.

Often revivals start with a breakthrough in one of these areas. But to endure—to mature into a lasting move of God—Choung and Pfeiffer contend that revival must bring together Word, deed, and power, all grounded in love.

As Paul reminded us in 1 Corinthians 13, even if we prophesy or perform miracles, without love we are nothing. Revival is not about spiritual spectacle—it's about deeper roots in Christ.

And here's what we must never forget:

- Revival isn't manufactured.
- It's not something we work up.
- It's something God sends down.

As Peter Lewis said, "Committees cannot organize it; festivals and celebrations cannot duplicate it; we cannot work it up: only God can send it down."[4]

But God doesn't send revival into thin air. He sends it into prepared hearts. He sends it where conviction softens pride, where repentance clears the ground, where resilience builds roots deep enough to carry what heaven wants to pour out.

THREE MARKS OF REVIVAL

Every revival—no matter the time, the place, or the people—shares three unmistakable marks. These are not techniques. They are signs the ground has been prepared, the rain is falling, and the Spirit is moving.

- A profound longing for God
- A renewed conviction of sin
- A noticeable outpouring of the Spirit

These three attributes grow best in lives where the lies of the enemy have been exposed and defeated.

A Profound Longing

If we long for revival, we must hunger for God's truth, humble ourselves, and prepare our hearts for the rain He is ready to send.

Revival begins where human striving ends. It begins with a holy hunger—not for more success, not just for personal breakthrough, but for the presence of God Himself.

The psalmist cried, "Will *you* not revive us again?" (Psalm 85:6)—not "How can we revive ourselves?" True revival begins not with our effort but with our desperation.

This kind of longing redirects our attention from self to God. It dethrones busyness, performance, and distraction. It places Jesus back at the center. It's not just spiritual experience we crave—it's the glory of the living God.

We see this kind of longing after the exile, when a small remnant of Israelites returned to a ruined Jerusalem. Babylon had been comfortable—prosperous, familiar. But Jerusalem was a pile of rubble, economically devastated, socially unstable, and spiritually barren. Many of the exiles chose to remain in Babylon, preferring its safety to the sacrifice required to rebuild. Yet a few—the ones with a holy hunger—chose the harder road. They returned to the ruins, believing that even broken stones were better than distant comforts if it meant being close to the promises of God.

It was in that setting of discouragement and devastation that the Sons of Korah cried out, "Will you not revive us again, that your people may rejoice in you?" (Psalm 85:6). They weren't asking for better circumstances. They were pleading for God's presence to be restored among them.

That is where revival always begins. Not with strength. Not with strategy. But with desperate, unyielding hunger for God to move again.

In seasons of true revival, prayer becomes not a duty but a lifeline. Worship becomes not a routine but a cry of the heart. The longing for God's presence outweighs every other pursuit.

Revival doesn't erupt among the casually curious. It breaks out among the spiritually desperate.

A Conviction of Sin

Longing alone is not enough.

The second mark of revival is a profound conviction of sin paired with a deep awareness of God's love and presence.

In 1949, on the Isle of Lewis in the Hebrides, two women in their eighties—one of them blind—were burdened by the spiritual state of their church. Not a single young person was part of their congregation, so they began to pray twice a week, often from ten o'clock at night until three or four in the morning.

As they prayed, one of them received a vision of their church packed with young people. They called their pastor about it and challenged him to host his own prayer meeting at the same times—Tuesday and Friday nights. He accepted and started to pray with seven men.

After a month and a half, a young deacon stood up in the church and read this passage:

Who may ascend into the hill of the LORD?
Or who may stand in His holy place?
He who has clean hands and a pure heart,
Who has not lifted up his soul to an idol,
Nor sworn deceitfully.
He shall receive blessing from the LORD. (Psalm 24:3–5, NKJV)

Then he closed his Bible, and looking down, the deacon said these words straight from his heart: "It seems to me to be much humbug to be praying as we are praying, to be waiting as we are waiting, if we ourselves are not rightly related to God."[5]

Then he lifted his hands. And with a trembling voice, he cried out, "God, are my hands clean? Is my heart pure?" Then he fell into a trance.

Conviction hit the room. And the power of God swept in. Later, at a nearby dance hall, the presence of God would move in such a dramatic fashion that the music stopped, and in minutes the hall emptied of its one hundred or so young people, and they all went to the church. Soon after, eight hundred poured into this church and prayed until four in the morning.

The revival would last for three more years.

Revival always begins in the heart—with prayer, with confession, with a deep awareness of the presence of God, and a strong conviction that we don't deserve it. That if God kept a record of sin, who could stand before the Lord?[6]

Revival in the Hebrides didn't start with a better strategy, it started with a broken heart.

As Charles Finney says, "A revival always includes conviction of sin on the part of the church. . . . Backslidden Christians will be brought to repentance. A revival is nothing else than a new beginning of obedience to God."[7]

Not guilt-driven obedience, but Spirit-filled delight in living for Christ.

When revival comes, even the "small" sins no longer seem small. Self-righteousness crumbles. Self-pity melts away. The need to control our image before others disappears. We confess not based on how we think others will respond, but because we are amazed that a holy God would meet us in mercy.

Conviction of sin is not condemnation. It's the doorway to freedom.

A Noticeable Outpouring

Revival is never hidden. It leaves evidence. It demands attention. People notice.

In Acts 2, the crowd thought the disciples were drunk because of the power and passion they witnessed. Peter stood up and preached—and three thousand repented and believed. In Acts 4, when the believers prayed, the place was shaken. In Acts 10, the Spirit visibly fell on Gentiles, and even skeptics couldn't deny what they saw. It was noticeable.

Revival should be visible in our lives—how we speak, how we give, how we forgive.

The famous evangelist and founder of Methodism, John Wesley, did not have a very fruitful ministry in the United States early on. He returned to the UK discouraged. But he had an encounter with God on May 24, 1738, in London at Aldersgate that forever changed him. He wrote, "I felt my heart strangely warmed. I felt I did trust in Christ, Christ alone for salvation; and an assurance was given me, that he had taken away my sins, even mine, and saved me from the law of sin and death."[8]

Wesley had been a Christian before Aldersgate—but after that night he was never the same. His preaching carried a new depth. His ministry bore a new kind of fruit. He became so instrumental in the First Great Awakening that it helped lay the spiritual foundation for a new nation—one built on religious freedom, checks and balances, and a sober understanding of human depravity and our need for God.

The point here is that when the Spirit falls upon people and upon congregations, they are transformed. It is undeniable to those who experience it, and unmistakable to those who witness it. The signs may look different in every generation, but the change is real. It doesn't always have to be loud or in your face. But you can look and say that person is different. There is evidence—in the depth of worship, in the intentionality of Christ-centered community, and with tangible acts of justice.

Revival should be visible in our lives—how we speak, how we give, how we forgive. It should show up in how we practice hospitality, how we show courage, and how we bear witness.

People should see the difference. They may not understand it, but they should feel it. Revival is magnetic. It's holy. It's real.

REVIVAL IMAGINED: THE MIRACLE HIDDEN JUST BENEATH THE SURFACE

I want you to go with me for a minute to the Atacama Desert in Chile, the driest place on earth. It's the kind of place where you wonder how anything survives . . . because very few things do.

The Atacama Desert receives less than half an inch of rain each year. But a few years ago, something miraculous happened: a downpour—a flood years in the making. When this happens, the Atacama can receive seven years' worth of rain in just twelve hours. Water seeps into the dry desert cracks and finds something hidden beneath, waiting for this very moment: seeds. Thousands upon thousands of them bide their time, waiting for what is known as a *superbloom.*

When the rain fell, more than two hundred species of flowers bloomed at once, covering the desert with a flood of color as far as the eye could see. Barrenness was replaced with brilliance. Desolation gave way to life.

Revival is beneath the surface of our culture right now. The ground feels hard and dry, but there is the potential for something miraculous waiting beneath the hard exterior. The seeds are ready. We just need the rain. Despite all we see, the kingdom is at hand. It is in our midst just beneath the surface.

Isaiah prophesied, "You heavens above, rain down my righteousness; let the clouds shower it down. Let the earth open wide, let salvation spring up, let righteousness flourish with it; I, the Lord, have created it" (Isaiah 45:8).

Imagine with me a generation marked not by compromise

but by courage. A generation done with shallow religion and hungry for the real thing. A generation tired of division, longing for the presence of God. A generation no longer chasing personal comfort or clinging to memories of the past, but believing that the same Spirit who moved in Acts can move again today.

Imagine with me a generation who takes up the mantle to live holy lives in an unholy world, to love their enemies when cancel culture demands they cut them off, to carry truth and grace into every sphere of influence—arts, education, politics, business, technology, media, and the church.

Imagine neighborhoods coming alive with prayer. Churches filled again with worship and repentance. Justice ministries started not in conference rooms but in living rooms—spontaneous, Spirit-led, sacrificial. Imagine marriages healed. Addictions broken. Foster care waitlists reversed. Communities renewed.

Imagine churches known for downloading the sound of heaven and singing it boldly over an anxious generation. Imagine believers giving sacrificially, forgiving relentlessly, serving fearlessly, and loving unconditionally.

Imagine revival not as something we remember from the past but something we carry into the future. Imagine historians and secular journalists trying to explain the inexplicable: how a humble, Spirit-filled generation reshaped every sector of society by simply living surrendered lives.

Imagine schools teaching character rooted in the gospel. Fathers reuniting with their children. Businesses transformed into kingdom enterprises. Mainstream media telling stories of redemption and restoration. Even politics shifting—justice and righteousness becoming the rallying cry once again.

Imagine the light of Christ shining in a world growing

darker—and a generation rising to shine that light without fear or apology.

The invitation is clear: Keep planting the seeds of revival in your own heart—through worship that starts with God, commitment to the local church, deep engagement with Scripture, bold public witness, justice rooted in the cross, Spirit-filled surrender, and forgiveness shaped by enemy love.

The days of testing are not just coming—they are already here in so many ways. Your job is to stand strong, to discern the truth from the lies, and to recognize when what sounds like truth departs from the narrow way.

REVIVAL EMBODIED: LIVING WITH RESILIENCE IN A COMPROMISED AGE

If we can let God's truth take root in us, there's no telling how revival might break through the hardened soil of our secular age.

I vividly remember when God first called me into ministry. I was just fifteen, on a mission trip to Belize, when I felt the nudge of the Spirit, and yet fear rose up in me quickly.

So I made a deal with God: "Lord, I will go anywhere and do anything . . . but please don't ever ask me to speak in public."

The idea of preaching terrified me. My thoughts moved too fast. I didn't think I was articulate enough. I was comfortable serving behind the scenes—encouraging, counseling, helping others—but putting words together in front of people? That felt impossible.

I said no.

I assumed public speaking was for someone else—someone bolder, smarter, more gifted.

But God didn't listen to my excuses.

Instead, He pushed me forward. Sometimes gently. Sometimes dragging me by the collar. And today, I'm writing this to you as proof that God's power is made perfect in weakness (2 Corinthians 12:9).

The enemy wanted me to doubt myself. To stay silent. To believe I was unqualified.

But God had a different plan.

And I believe He has a different plan for you too.

God doesn't call the equipped—He equips the called.

What might He be calling you to do?

Maybe He is stirring your heart to start a ministry. Maybe He's calling you to mentor someone younger in the faith. Maybe He is asking you to open your home to a foster child. Maybe it's time to say yes to leading a small group. Or to a bold new step in your workplace or community.

Whatever it is, you probably already know. Even if it looks crazy on paper, something inside you won't let it go. That's how you know it's from God.

The truth is, God takes ordinary people and *expands their capacity* to do extraordinary things. I've seen it in my life. I've seen it in the lives of those around me. He doesn't choose the strongest, most gifted, or most impressive. He chooses those who know they need Him—because they'll have no choice but to rely on Him:

> My grace is sufficient for you, for my power is made perfect in weakness. (2 Corinthians 12:9)

Maybe the thing that makes you feel least qualified is the very thing God wants to use. Your inadequacy might be your greatest qualification.

And that kind of obedience—saying yes when it costs you—is exactly what our generation is being called to now.

God doesn't call the equipped—He equips the called.

All throughout history, God has used moments like this to refine His people. To distinguish between those who simply wear the label "Christian" and those who live it—daily, courageously, sacrificially.

In a strange way, the growing hostility to biblical faith is actually helping. It's burning away cultural Christianity. It's revealing who's in and who's out. Those who are drifting, deconstructing, or disengaging from faith have a short window to make up their mind who they will serve. They will not be able to stand much longer in this sea of secularism.

Jesus warned that this deception would happen. In Matthew 7, He spoke about *false prophets.* He wasn't describing outsiders. He was talking about *insiders*—people who speak the language of faith but twist the truth to fit their desires. Those who sound spiritual but live with no real surrender. People who preach tolerance but never call for repentance. Who know how to speak of love but quietly mock the authority of Scripture.

That's the kind of drift we're seeing today. And not just out in the world, but inside the church.

These voices don't always sound heretical. That's what makes them dangerous. They sound wise. Nuanced. Compassionate. But over time, they lead people away from the narrow path. And here's the sobering part: It's often not intentional. The slide into false teaching rarely begins with rebellion. It begins with reluctance. A reluctance to say what's true because we don't want to offend. A reluctance to believe that God's Word is still trustworthy. A reluctance to draw a line when culture demands we blur it.

And slowly but surely, we trade clarity for confusion.

But I have good news: Revival has always come when the church regains her clarity. When we return to what is true, what is right, what is holy—not in anger or arrogance, but in humility and surrender. We don't need louder voices. We need deeper roots.

REVIVAL STARTS HERE: SAYING YES TO GOD'S INVITATION

Revival doesn't stay in the sanctuary. It spills into the streets. It moves from the prayer room to the living room, from the altar to the classroom, from the gathering to the marketplace. And it doesn't move through big programs or personalities—it moves through people. Ordinary men and women who carry the extraordinary presence of God into their everyday lives.

Revival is not just something you attend, it's something you embody. It's seen in the resilience of your faith when others fall away. It's seen in your joy when cynicism is easier, in your humility when pride would be safer, in your forgiveness when cancel culture demands revenge, and in your surrender when self-promotion would be applauded.

You weren't created to stand on the sidelines. You were created to carry the light of Christ into a world that desperately needs it. The light Jesus placed inside you is not meant to be covered by fear, compromise, or cultural conformity. It's meant to shine brightly—especially in times like these.

The call is simple, but it will cost everything. It calls for worship that starts with God, not self. It calls for commitment to the local church, even when it's costly. It calls for bold public witness, even when it's unpopular. It calls for deep engagement with Scripture, even when it confronts. It calls for justice rooted in the cross, not in outrage. It calls for Spirit-filled surrender, even when it feels foolish. It calls for forgiveness that refuses to cancel those God came to redeem.

Every time you choose this path, you become a bearer of revival. Every time you say no to the lies of the enemy and yes to the practices of Jesus, you make space for the Spirit to move—first in you, then through you.

Revival doesn't begin somewhere out there. It begins here. Now. In hearts willing to say yes. It may begin unseen. It may begin small. But it never stays that way. Because when the Spirit breathes on surrendered lives, what seems small becomes unshakable—rooted, resilient, and impossible to ignore.

The author of Hebrews warns that "only *unshakable* things will remain." But then challenges us: "Since we are receiving a Kingdom that is *unshakable,* let us be thankful and please God by worshiping him with holy fear and awe" (12:27–28, NLT).

This is your moment—not to drift, but to stand firm. Not to shrink back, but to rise up. Not to be discipled by the culture, but to confront it with the truth of the gospel.

The seeds have already been planted. The rain is already starting to fall.

The only question left is: Are you ready? Will you say yes?

ACKNOWLEDGMENTS

First and foremost, I thank God for giving me the burden to write this book and for the grace to see it through. His power continues to be made perfect in my weakness.

To the people of The District Church—you have shaped every page of this book with your faith, your questions, and your perseverance in the gospel. My prayer has always been that this book would be a blessing to you and to those you are trying to reach.

To my team who have walked with me through this entire process:

To Madeline McIntosh and Tina Constable, who believed in this message—and in me—before I had written a word.

To Bryan Norman at Alive Literary, who took a chance on a non-platformed, no-name, first-time author—thank you for your friendship, encouragement, and coaching.

To Drew Dixon, my editor, who has been with me every step of the way, reading early drafts and pushing me to show, not just tell, both the problem and the solution. I'm grateful for your patience and guidance as I navigated this process for the first time.

To Campbell Wharton—your confidence in me and this project has meant more than you know.

To Mark Batterson, whose love for writing is contagious and whose encouragement and counsel throughout this process have been incredible.

To Jenn Jennings, my incredible assistant, who helped manage my schedule and competing priorities so I could actually finish. To Yohan Perera and Savannah Montgomery—thank you for helping me stay connected to the heart and voice of the next generation.

To those who read early drafts and offered invaluable feedback—Pastor Rich Nathan, Pastor Stuart McAlpine, Scott Garber, Chris Backert, Eliot Ritzema—thank you for sharpening my thinking.

To Jack Durham—thank you for being a champion of this project from the beginning, and for helping shape my writing and its connection to young adults.

To Pastor Kevin Nderitu and Pastor Brian Carrier—your senior leadership at The District Church gave me the space to reflect, pray, and write about what we are facing in the wider culture. Thank you for carrying the weight of the day-to-day with faith and vision.

To Pastor Don Coleman and Pastor Stuart Royall—thank you for your spiritual covering since my college days. Your faithful prayers and prophetic encouragement have helped keep me grounded throughout this writing journey.

To my Mom and Dad—thank you for your lifelong support and for believing in my call to ministry, even when it didn't follow the conventional path. Your faith and sacrifice have laid the foundation for everything I do.

To Amy, my best friend and partner in life and ministry—thank you for your unwavering support in this book project. You have been my number one encourager and the first to give me feedback on nearly every word. Your faith and strength have been a rock, and your influence is woven throughout these pages.

To Elijah and Natalie—thank you for your patience and joy.

Your hugs and laughter remind me every day of what matters most.

And to the many friends not named here—the unseen prayer warriors—you have labored with me. This is our offering together.

APPENDIX

These seven lies represent some of the most common and corrosive lies shaping Christian faith today—not just in urban centers like where I live, but across the nation and beyond.

Through the internet and digital culture, progressive secular values have been exported everywhere. Geographic boundaries have collapsed. The pressure to drift is no longer localized; it is global.

SEVEN LIES CHRISTIANS BELIEVE

Lie 1: It's All About Me
Lie 2: Church Is Optional
Lie 3: Faith Is Private
Lie 4: The Bible Is Outdated
Lie 5: Charity Is Enough
Lie 6: Everything Is Rational
Lie 7: Enemies Must Be Canceled

We must be discerning, because without discernment, we inevitably drift toward counterfeit identities. That has been Satan's strategy from the beginning—to attack our identity in Christ.

In the garden, the enemy whispered, "Did God really say?" and planted doubt. Then he offered the ultimate lie: "If you do this, you will be like God."

The same strategy still works today. If the enemy can distort what we believe about God and about ourselves, he can derail our calling before it ever takes root.

COUNTERFEIT IDENTITIES

1: The Self-Centered Worshiper
2: The Church Shopper
3: The Lukewarm Believer
4: The Selective Christian
5: The Armchair Activist
6: The Skeptical Believer
7: The Divisive Influencer

But here is the invitation—the hopeful call at the heart of it all. These are the core spiritual practices that have sustained faithful, Bible-believing churches throughout every generation.

HISTORIC SPIRITUAL PRACTICES

1: **True Worship**—an invitation to a renewed and God-centered faith
2: **Deep Community**—an invitation to be spiritually formed through the local church
3: **Bold Storytelling**—an invitation to share your faith with courage and authenticity
4: **Bible Engagement**—an invitation to dive deep into all of God's Word
5: **Biblical Justice**—an invitation to pursue justice with sacrificial love
6: **Spirit-Filled Living**—an invitation to discover and operate in your spiritual gifts
7: **Radical Forgiveness**—an invitation to practice peacemaking in a divided world

Chapter	The Lie	Counterfeit Identity	The Commitment
1	It's All About Me	The Self-Centered Worshiper	True Worship
2	Church Is Optional	The Church Shopper	Deep Community
3	Faith Is Private	The Lukewarm Believer	Bold Storytelling
4	The Bible Is Outdated	The Selective Christian	Bible Engagement
5	Charity Is Enough	The Armchair Activist	Biblical Justice
6	Everything Is Rational	The Skeptical Believer	Spirit-Filled Living
7	Enemies Must Be Canceled	The Divisive Influencer	Radical Forgive-ness

DISCUSSION AND REFLECTION QUESTIONS

Lie 1: It's All About Me

- What are some ways our culture encourages us to make faith more about personal fulfillment than about God's glory?
- How does re-centering our worship on God, rather than ourselves, deepen our relationship with Him?

Lie 2: Church Is Optional

- What role has the local church played in your spiritual growth? Have you ever been tempted to treat church as optional instead of essential?
- How can we help those who are deconstructing their faith find a renewed and meaningful connection to the body of Christ?

Lie 3: Faith Is Private

- Why is it tempting to keep faith private instead of living as a bold public witness? How does that mindset affect our ability to share our story and the gospel with others?
- What are some practical ways you can make your faith visible in everyday conversations and relationships?

Lie 4: The Bible Is Outdated

- Have you encountered people who believe the Bible is outdated or irrelevant? How do you respond to those beliefs?
- What are some ways we can help others see the timeless relevance and authority of God's Word?

Lie 5: Charity Is Enough

- How does biblical justice go deeper than charity or worldly activism? What does it look like to pursue justice rooted in the gospel through sacrificial love?
- How can practicing relational generosity change the way we engage injustice in our communities?

Lie 6: Everything Is Rational

- How do we balance the desire to understand the world with the need for faith in the unseen and miraculous? Have you ever struggled with skepticism in your walk with God?
- How can we create more space for the supernatural work of the Spirit in our daily lives and ministries?

Lie 7: Enemies Must Be Canceled

- How does the spirit of "cancel culture" show up in our relationships, both inside and outside the church? Have you ever struggled to forgive someone who disagreed with you or hurt you?

- What are practical ways we can pursue peace and reconciliation with those who hold different beliefs or views?

APPLICATION TO DAILY LIFE AND MINISTRY

Identifying Counterfeit Identities

- Which counterfeit identity do you find most challenging personally, and why?
- How can others in your group or community support you as you seek to reject that counterfeit identity and live in your true identity in Christ?

The Role of the Church

- What role does the church play in helping you combat these lies?
- How does being actively involved in worship, community, discipleship, and Scripture strengthen your ability to stand firm in the truth?
- How can we, as a church, become more proactive in exposing lies and cultivating truth within our congregation and community?

PERSONAL COMMITMENT

Historic Practices

- Which of the seven historic practices do you sense God calling you to strengthen in this season?
- What is one concrete step you can take this week to move deeper into that practice?

NOTES

WHEN TRUTH GETS TWISTED

1. Jim Davis and Michael Graham, *The Great Dechurching: Who's Leaving, Why Are They Going, and What Will It Take to Bring Them Back?* (Zondervan, 2023).
2. D. Martin Lloyd-Jones, *Studies in the Sermon on the Mount* (William B. Eerdmans, 1960), 497–506.
3. Robert Bellah et al., *Habits of the Heart: Individualism and Commitment in American Life* (University of California Press, 1985), 89.
4. Amy Wallace, "The Beyonc Outtakes," *GQ*, January 22, 2013, gq.com/story/beyonce-cover-story-outtakes-gq-february-2013.
5. Joel Osteen, *Your Best Life Now: 7 Steps to Living at Your Full Potential* (FaithWords, 2004), 103.
6. Glennon Doyle, *Untamed* (The Dial Press, 2020), 122.
7. Mark Sayers, *Disappearing Church: From Cultural Relevance to Gospel Resilience* (Moody, 2016).
8. Philip Rieff, *The Triumph of the Therapeutic: Uses of Faith After Freud* (Harper & Row, 1966).
9. Carl Trueman is one of the more recent authors who have adapted Philip Rieff's framework into a more popularized "Three Cultures" version to explain the cultural shifts today. Carl R. Trueman, *The Rise and Triumph of the Modern Self: Cultural Amnesia, Expressive Individualism, and the Road to Sexual Revolution* (Crossway, 2020), 37–42.
10. Sayers, *Disappearing Church*, 47.
11. John Mark Comer, "Where Can Progressive Christianity Lead?," ThinQ Media, YouTube video, December 1, 2021, youtube.com/watch?v=PVlU7uFsuXQ.
12. Roger Olson, *Against Liberal Theology: Putting the Brakes on Progressive Christianity* (Zondervan, 2022).

13. Roger Olson, *The Journey of Modern Theology: From Reconstruction to Deconstruction* (InterVarsity Press Academic, 2013).
14. Olson, *The Journey of Modern Theology,* 30.
15. H. Richard Niebuhr, *Christ and Culture* (Harper & Row, 1951).
16. 1 John 4:4.

1: WHEN DEVOTION DRIFTS

1. C. S. Lewis, *The Screwtape Letters* (HarperOne, 1996), letter 4, 15–16.
2. Julianne Holt-Lunstad et al., "Social Relationships and Mortality Risk: A Meta-analytic Review," *PLoS Medicine* 7, no. 7 (2010): e1000316.
3. Jacob Sweet, "The Loneliness Pandemic," *Harvard Magazine,* January-February 2021, harvardmagazine.com/2020/12/feature-the-loneliness-pandemic.
4. Giselle Abramovich, "Redefining health through vitality: New insight into five years of loneliness trends," 2024, newsroom.thecignagroup.com/vitality-research-new-insight-into-five-years-of-loneliness.
5. Office of the U.S. Surgeon General, *Our Epidemic of Loneliness and Isolation: The U.S. Surgeon General's Advisory on the Healing Effects of Social Connection and Community* (U.S. Department of Health and Human Services, 2023), 9.
6. Exodus 3:2–5.
7. Lewis, *The Screwtape Letters,* letter 12, 57–58.
8. "The Outpouring at Asbury University," Asbury University, asbury.edu/outpouring.

2: WHEN CHURCH FEELS OPTIONAL

1. Jim Davis and Michael Graham, *The Great Dechurching: Who's Leaving, Why Are They Going, and What Will It Take to Bring Them Back?* (Zondervan, 2023), 5.
2. Davis and Graham, *The Great Dechurching,* 3.
3. Davis and Graham, *The Great Dechurching,* 3.
4. "Doubt and Faith: Top Reasons People Question Christianity," *Barna Group,* updated March 1, 2023, barna.com/research/doubt-faith.

5. "Unveiling the Exodus: Americans' Reasons for Leaving Religious Traditions," Public Religion Research Institute, July 21, 2023, prri.org/spotlight/unveiling-the-exodus-americans-reasons-for-leaving-religious-traditions.
6. "Why Americans Go (and Don't Go) to Religious Services," Pew Research Center, August 1, 2018, pewresearch.org/religion/2018/08/01/why-americans-go-to-religious-services.
7. Davis and Graham, *The Great Dechurching,* 61.
8. C. S. Lewis, *The Screwtape Letters* (HarperOne, 1996), letter 16, 81–82.
9. More than 380 million Christians throughout the world suffer high levels of persecution and discrimination for their faith and are not able to worship freely. "World Watch List 2025," Open Doors, opendoors.org/en-US/persecution/countries.
10. *Strong's Concordance,* s.v. "ekklésia," Bible Hub, biblehub.com/greek/1577.htm.
11. Lauren Jackson, "Americans Haven't Found a Satisfying Alternative to Religion," *New York Times,* April 18, 2025, nytimes.com/2025/04/18/style/religion-america.html.
12. "Religion's Relationship to Happiness, Civic Engagement and Health Around the World," Pew Research Center, January 31, 2019, pewresearch.org/religion/2019/01/31/religions-relationship-to-happiness-civic-engagement-and-health-around-the-world.
13. Tyler J. VanderWeele et al., "Association of Religious Service Attendance with Mortality Among Women," *JAMA Internal Medicine* 176, no. 6 (2016): 777–85, doi.org/10.1001/jamainternmed.2016.1615.
14. Matthew 18:20; Acts 2:42–47; 1 Corinthians 12:27; Hebrews 10:24–25.
15. Matthew 24:24.
16. Matthew 7:15–20.
17. Ephesians 5:26–27.
18. John 1:29.

3: WHEN FAITH BECOMES PRIVATE

1. Matthew 10:11–13; Luke 10:5–7.
2. Michael Paulson, "Ma Siss's Place: The Birth of a Church," *The Boston Globe,* December 23, 2007, bostonglobe.com/

metro/2007/12/23/from-dorchester-chop-shop-place-pray/aoYf8qe43vYNQrUTMnF3mI/story.html.

3. Revelation 2 and 3.
4. Craig S. Keener, *The IVP Bible Background Commentary: New Testament,* 2nd ed. (InterVarsity Press Academic, 2014), 736–37.

   Grant R. Osborne, *Revelation: Verse by Verse,* Osborne New Testament Commentaries (Lexham Press, 2016), 91.
5. "The Martyrdom of Polycarp 9.3," in *The Apostolic Fathers,* ed. and trans. Michael W. Holmes, Third Edition (Baker Academic, 2007), 318.
6. C. S. Lewis, *The Screwtape Letters* (HarperOne, 1996), letter 23, 126.
7. Kenton Beshore and Muriithi Wanjau, *Rooted: Connect with God, the Church, Your Purpose* (Mariners Church, 2020).
8. *Theological Dictionary of the New Testament,* eds. Gerhard Kittel and Gerhard Friedrich, trans. Geoffrey Bromiley (William B. Eerdmans, 1968), 474–514.

4: WHEN THE BIBLE GETS EDITED

1. Krista Tippett, "The New Evangelical Leaders: Part 1," On Being, November 29, 2007, onbeing.org/programs/jim-wallis-the-new-evangelical-leaders-part-i.
2. Matthew 5:28.
3. Romans 1:18–27.
4. 1 Corinthians 6:9–10; 18–20.
5. C. S. Lewis, *The Screwtape Letters* (HarperOne, 1996), letter 1, 1.
6. David Kinnaman, "Competing Worldviews Influence Today's Christians," Barna Group, May 9, 2017. barna.com/research/competing-worldviews-influence-todays-christians.
7. David Kinnaman, "Almost Half of Practicing Christian Millennials Say Evangelism Is Wrong," Barna Group, February 5, 2019, barna.com/research/millennials-oppose-evangelism.
8. 1 Corinthians 1:17.
9. Matthew 25:31–46.
10. For further reading on how secular culture has given rise to expressive individualism and the autonomous self, check out Carl Trueman, *The Rise and Triumph of the Modern Self* (Crossway,

2020); Charles Taylor, *A Secular Age* (Belknap Press of Harvard University Press, 2007).

11. Alan Shlemon, "Marriage Doctrine Alone Disqualifies Pro-Gay Theology," Stand to Reason, March 28, 2017, str.org/w/marriage-doctrine-alone-disqualifies-pro-gay-theology.
12. "Faith Positions," Human Rights Campaign, hrc.org/resources/faith-positions.
13. The Wesleyan Quadrilateral articulates this argument further, highlighting how John Wesley utilized Scripture, Tradition, Reason, and Experience in his theological method and ultimately was guided by Scripture. Albert C. Outler, *John Wesley's Sermons: An Anthology* (Abingdon Press, 1991), 22.
14. John 1:1, 14.
15. Ephesians 4:11–16.
16. Acts 2:42.
17. Isaiah 55:10–11.
18. "Best-selling book of non-fiction," Guinness World Records, guinnessworldrecords.com/world-records/best-selling-book-of-non-fiction.
19. "State of the Bible 2021: Five Key Findings" Barna Group, May 19, 2021, barna.com/research/sotb-2021.
20. "Bible Engagement and 'the Power of 4,'" Center for Bible Engagement (Our Daily Bread Ministries), 2024, centerforbibleengagement.org/_files/ugd/aae503_e0a7c3d59fbc4c93b55e7268d868de2e.pdf.
21. James E. Short, "How Much Media? 2013 Report on American Consumers," (University of Southern California, 2013), 7, business.tivo.com/content/dam/tivo/resources/tivo-HMM-Consumer-Report-2013_Release.pdf.
22. Dave Chaffey, "Global Social Media Statistics Research Summary 2025," Smart Insights, updated January 22, 2025, smartinsights.com/social-media-marketing/social-media-strategy/new-global-social-media-research.
23. Nicholas Carr, *The Shallows: What the Internet is Doing to Our Brains,* (W. W. Norton & Company, 2011).
24. "People Who Regularly Read Bible Say It's Better Than Coffee to

Jump-Start Their Mornings," American Bible Society, May 8, 2018, americanbible.org/press-release/people-who-regularly-read-bible-say-its-better-than-coffee-to-jump-start-th.

5: WHEN JUSTICE GETS HIJACKED

1. Jedd Medefind, *Becoming Home: Adoption, Foster Care, and Mentoring—Living Out God's Heart for Orphans* (Zondervan, 2014).
2. DC127, dc127.org.
3. Tanya de Sousa and Meghan Henry, "The 2024 Annual Homelessness Assessment Report (AHAR) to Congress," U.S. Department of Housing and Urban Development, December 2024, huduser.gov/portal/sites/default/files/pdf/2024-AHAR-Part-1.pdf.
4. Emily Shrider, "Poverty in the United States: 2023," United States Census Bureau, September 2024, census.gov/library/publications/2024/demo/p60-283.html.
5. Briana Sullivan et al., "Wealth by Race of Householder," United States Census Bureau, April 23, 2024, census.gov/library/stories/2024/04/wealth-by-race.html.
6. "50 Million People Worldwide in Modern Slavery," International Labour Organization, September 12, 2022, ilo.org/resource/news/50-million-people-worldwide-modern-slavery.
7. "World Watch List 2025," Open Doors, opendoors.org/en-US/persecution/countries.
8. "Abortion in the United States," Guttmacher Institute, April 2025, guttmacher.org/fact-sheet/induced-abortion-united-states.
9. "Abortion," World Health Organization, May 17, 2024, who.int/news-room/fact-sheets/detail/abortion.
10. A. B. Franzen, "Reading the Bible in America: The Moral and Political Attitude Effect," *Review of Religious Research* 55, no. 3 (2013): 393–411, doi.org/10.1007/s13644-013-0109-2.
11. R. J. Ridder et al., "Increased Bible Reading, Religious Beliefs, and Prosociality During College," *Review of Religious Research* 66, no. 3 (2024): 260–79, doi.org/10.1177/0034673X241256281.
12. Dr. King addressed the issue of why being a good Samaritan sometimes isn't enough in his famous speech "A Time to Break

Silence," which he gave exactly a year before his death, on April 4, 1967.

13. John Perkins, *Beyond Charity: The Call to Christian Community Development* (Baker Books, 1993).
14. David Brooks, *Bobos in Paradise: The New Upper Class and How They Got There* (Simon & Schuster, 2000).
15. C. S. Lewis, *The Screwtape Letters* (HarperOne, 1996), Letter 13, 67.
16. Jesus' words in Matthew 25 infer that true believers would be able to produce this letter of reference on Judgment Day.
17. Romans 3:23.
18. Jeremiah 17:9.
19. Matthew 6:10.
20. C. S. Lewis, *Mere Christianity* (HarperOne, 2001), 134.
21. Exodus 22:21–27.
22. Leviticus 19:9–10.
23. Deuteronomy 24:14–15.
24. Exodus 20:3.
25. Exodus 20:4–5.
26. Exodus 3:7.
27. Isaiah 1:16–17.
28. Isaiah 58:6–7.
29. Amos 5:24.
30. Micah 6:8.
31. Psalm 82:3–4.
32. Proverbs 14:31.
33. Proverbs 31:8–9.
34. Luke 4:16–21.
35. Luke 6:20–23.
36. Luke 10:25–37.
37. Mark 10:17–31.
38. 2 Corinthians 8:9.
39. Luke 9:58.
40. Acts 2:44–45.
41. Acts 4:32–35.
42. Acts 6:1–7.
43. Galatians 2:10.

44. 1 John 3:17–18.
45. *The Poverty & Justice Bible,* Contemporary English Version (American Bible Society, 2009).
46. "Under-five Mortality," UNICEF, March 2025, data.unicef.org/topic/child-survival/under-five-mortality.
47. Hannah Ritchie et al., "Population Growth," Our World in Data, 2023, ourworldindata.org/population-growth.
48. Psalm 74:1–4; Romans 13:1–7.
49. Thaddeus J. Williams, *Confronting Injustice Without Compromising Truth: 12 Questions Christians Should Ask About Social Justice* (Zondervan, 2020), 4–5, 162–164. In these pages, Williams distinguishes between Social Justice A, a biblically grounded approach to justice rooted in Scripture, and Social Justice B, justice movements shaped by secular ideologies such as Marxism and postmodern critical theory.
50. David Brooks, *How to Know a Person: The Art of Seeing Others Deeply and Being Deeply Seen* (Random House, 2023), 101.
51. Henry D. Rack, *Reasonable Enthusiast: John Wesley and the Rise of Methodism* (Epworth Press, 1989), 363.
52. Bishop Kenneth L. Carder, "John Wesley on Giving," from the *Giving and the Gospel Symposium* (1997) and the United Methodist Summit on Christian Stewardship (2003), resourceumc.org/en/content/john-wesley-on-giving.
53. This phrase is often attributed to Mother Teresa.

6: WHEN REASON REPLACES REVELATION

1. Jeff Clabaugh, "Arlington Tops List of 'Most Educated' Cities (D.C. Is Close Behind)," WTOP News, October 17, 2023, wtop.com/business-finance/2023/10/arlington-is-most-educated-city-dc-is-close-behind.
2. Jesus said, "A time is coming and has now come when the true worshipers will worship the Father in the Spirit and in truth" (John 4:23).
3. Jesus taught that the most important command is: "Love the Lord your God with all your heart and with all your soul and with all your mind and with all your strength" (Mark 12:30).

4. John 4:23.
5. Proverbs 18:15.
6. Solomon said, "Trust in the Lord with all your heart and lean not on your own understanding" (Proverbs 3:5).
7. 1 Corinthians 2:16.
8. 1 Corinthians 2:16.
9. 1 Corinthians 2:9–10.
10. Colossians 2:6–10.
11. Aaron Earls, "9 Encouraging Trends for Global Christianity in 2025," Lifeway Research, February 11, 2025, research.lifeway.com/2025/02/11/9-encouraging-trends-for-global-christianity-in-2025.
12. "In U.S., Decline of Christianity Continues at Rapid Pace," Pew Research Center, October 17, 2019, pewresearch.org/religion/2019/10/17/in-u-s-decline-of-christianity-continues-at-rapid-pace.
    Philip Jenkins, *The Next Christendom: The Coming of Global Christianity,* Third Edition, (Oxford University Press, 2011).
    Todd M. Johnson and Gina A. Zurlo, *World Christian Encyclopedia,* Third Edition, (Edinburgh University Press, 2019).
13. Matthew 7:3–5.
14. The most comprehensive academic work on the historical case for the resurrection to date is N. T. Wright, *The Resurrection of the Son of God* (Fortress Press, 2003).
15. "All these are the work of one and the same Spirit, and he distributes them to each one, just as he determines" (1 Corinthians 12:11).
16. A. W. Tozer, attributed, in various compilations of his writings.

7: WHEN CONFLICT DIVIDES

1. "District of Columbia," 270 to Win, 270towin.com/states/district-of-columbia.
2. Saul Alinsky, *Rules for Radicals* (Random House, 1971), 130.
3. Alinsky, *Rules for Radicals,* 78.
4. C. S. Lewis, *The Screwtape Letters* (HarperOne, 1996), Letter 7, 34.
5. Samuel P. Jacobs, "Pastor Attacked for Anti-Gay Speech Pulls Out of Inauguration," *Reuters,* January 10, 2013, reuters.com/article/world/us-politics/pastor-attacked-for-anti-gay-speech-pulls-out-of-inauguration-idUSBRE90912G.

6. David Beasley, "Ousted Atlanta Fire Chief Files Federal Discrimination Complaint," *Religion News Service,* January 23, 2015, religionnews.com/2015/01/23/ousted-atlanta-fire-chief-files-federal-discrimination-complaint.
7. Benjamin Mays. "Eulogy for Dr. Martin Luther King, Jr.," Morehouse College, April 9, 1968.
8. Martin Luther King, Jr., *Strength to Love* (Harper & Row, 1963), 49.
9. Martin Luther King, Jr., "Loving Your Enemies," sermon, Dexter Avenue Baptist Church, Montgomery, AL, November 17, 1957.
10. Ephesians 6:12.
11. Augustine of Hippo, *Sermon 49: On the New Testament, in The Works of Saint Augustine: A Translation for the 21st Century,* trans. Edmund Hill, ed. John E. Rotelle (New City Press, 1990), Section 5.
12. Alfred Plummer, *An Exegetical Commentary on the Gospel According to S. Matthew,* (Paternoster, 1910), 89.
13. John Chrysostom, "Homilies of St. John Chrysostom, Archbishop of Constantinople on the Gospel according to St. Matthew," in *Saint Chrysostom: Homilies on the Gospel of Saint Matthew,* ed. Philip Schaff, trans. George Prevost and M. B. Riddle, Volume 10, A Select Library of the Nicene and Post-Nicene Fathers of the Christian Church, First Series (Christian Literature Company, 1888), 128.
14. Chrysostom, "Homilies" 126–28. 1) Do not take evil initiative. 2) Do not avenge another's evil. 3) Be quiet. 4) Suffer wrongly. 5) Surrender even more than demanded. 6) Do not hate. 7) Love. 8) Do good. 9) Entreat God on their behalf through prayer.
15. Ephesians 2:8–9.
16. Aaron Graham, "Overcoming Trauma and Finding Faith: The Transformative Story of Dieudonné Nahimana | EPISODE 07," The District Church, YouTube video, October 23, 2024, youtube.com/watch?v=AOC3r9l_r9g&t=1s.

8: JUST IMAGINE

1. Martyn Lloyd-Jones, *Revival* (Crossway, 1987), 99–100.
2. James Burns, *Revivals, Their Laws and Leaders* (Hodder and Stoughton, 1909), 1.

3. James Choung and Ryan Pfeiffer, *Longing for Revival: From Holy Discontent to Breakthrough Faith* (InterVarsity Press, 2020), 20–21.
4. Peter Lewis, Foreword to *Joy Unspeakable: Power and Renewal in the Holy Spirit,* by Martyn Lloyd-Jones (Harold Shaw, 1984), 9.
5. Duncan Campbell, *Revival in the Hebrides* (CreateSpace Independent Publishing Platform, 2016), 33–34.
6. Psalm 130:3–4.
7. Charles G. Finney, *Lectures on Revivals of Religion* (Baker Books, 1989), 12.
8. John Wesley, "The Journal of John Wesley, May 24, 1738," in *The Works of John Wesley,* 3rd ed., vol. 1 (Baker Book House, 1978), 103.

ABOUT THE AUTHOR

AARON GRAHAM is the founder and lead pastor of The District Church, a thriving multicultural congregation in Washington, D.C., representing more than eighty nations. For over fifteen years, he has pastored in the heart of the nation's capital, discipling a generation to follow Jesus with courage and conviction amid cultural compromise. He is currently leading an initiative to restore one of the city's most historic churches as a visible sign of the gospel's enduring presence in the heart of Washington, D.C.

Aaron earned a master's degree in public policy from Harvard's Kennedy School and a doctorate in missiology from Fuller Theological Seminary, where his studies focused on spiritual formation, cultural engagement, and the future of the church in the West. His ministry has been shaped by formative experiences as a missionary kid in Liberia and Kuwait—where he was held hostage during the Persian Gulf War—and by years spent living among the urban poor and pastoring an African American church plant in Boston.

He and his wife, Amy, are passionate advocates for foster care, adoption, and affordable housing. Together they founded DC127, a movement uniting churches to reverse the foster care waitlist. Aaron also serves on the mayor's faith advisory board and provides spiritual counsel to senior leaders in government, education, and business.

Aaron and Amy Graham live in Washington, D.C., with their two children, Elijah and Natalie.